Philippi at the
Time of Paul and
after His Death

Philippi at the Time of Paul and after His Death

Edited by
Charalambos Bakirtzis
and Helmut Koester

TRINITY PRESS INTERNATIONAL
Harrisburg, Pennsylvania

All photographs and line drawings are courtesy of Charalambos Bakirtzis and Chaido Koukouli-Chrysantaki.

Trinity Press International, P.O. Box 1321, Harrisburg, PA 17105
Trinity Press International is a division of the Morehouse Group

Library of Congress Cataloging-in-Publication Data

Philippi at the time of Paul and after his death / edited by
    Charalambos Bakirtzis and Helmut Koester.
        p.   cm.
    Includes bibliographical references and index.
    ISBN 1-56338-263-6 (pbk. : alk. paper)
    1. Philippi (Extinct city) 2. Christian antiquities – Greece –
Philippi (Extinct city) 3. Paul, the Apostle, Saint – Journeys –
Greece – Philippi (Extinct city) 4. Bible. N.T. Epistles of Paul –
Criticism, interpretation, etc. 5. Bible. N.T. Acts – Criticism,
interpretation, etc.   I. Bakirtzis, Ch. (Charalambos) II. Koester,
Helmut, 1926- .
    DF261.P53P45   1998
    939'.8 – dc21   98-39837

Printed in the United States of America

98 99 00 01 02   10 9 8 7 6 5 4 3 2 1

Contents

96401

Abbreviations

ADelt	*Archaeologikon Deltion*
AEphem	*Archaeologiki Ephemeris*
AJA	*American Journal of Archaeology*
AJP	*American Journal of Philology*
ANRW	*Aufstieg und Niedergang der römischen Welt*
ANSMN	*American Numismatic Society Museum Notes*
BCH	*Bulletin de Correspondance Hellénique*
BEvT	Beiträge zur evangelischen Theologie
CAH	*Cambridge Ancient History*
CB	*Cultura bíblica*
CII	*Corpus inscriptionum iudaicarum*
CIL	*Corpus inscriptionum latinarum*
CP	*Classical Philology*
DOP	Dumbarton Oaks Papers
EBib	Études bibliques
GGM	*Geographi Graeci minores*
HTR	*Harvard Theological Review*
IG	*Inscriptiones Graecae*
IGRR	*Inscriptiones Graecae ad Res Romanas Pertinentes*

JBR	*Journal of Bible and Religion*
JRS	*Journal of Roman Studies*
LCL	Loeb Classical Library
NovTSup	Novum Testamentum: Supplements
NRSV	New Revised Standard Version
NTS	*New Testament Studies*
PG	J. Migne, *Patrologia graeca*
PL	J. Migne, *Patrologia latina*
RHR	*Revue de l'histoire des religions*
SEG	*Supplementum Epigraphicum Graecum*
TAPA	*Transactions of the American Philological Association*
VC	*Vigiliae christianae*
ZPE	*Zeitschrift für Papyrologie und Epigraphik*

Short Titles

Actes du Xe Congrès International d'Archéologie Chrétienne

> *Actes du Xe Congrès International d'Archéologie Chrétienne, Thessalonique 28 Septembre–4 Octobre 1980* (Studi di Antichità Cristiana 37; Vatican City: Pontificio Istituto di Archeologia Cristiana; and Hellenika Supplementum 26; Thessalonike: Society for Macedonian Studies, 1984).

Bakalakis, "Neapolis, Christoupolis, Kavala"

> G. Bakalakis, "Neapolis, Christoupolis, Kavala," *AEphem* 1936, 1–46 [in Greek].

Bakirtzis, "The Day after the Destruction"

> Charalambos Bakirtzis, "The Day after the Destruction of Philippi," in *Proceedings of the First International Symposium on "Everyday Life in Byzantium," Athens 15–17 September 1988* (Athens: Center for Byzantine Research/E.I.E., 1989) 709 [in Greek].

Bormann, *Philippi*

> Lukas Bormann, *Philippi: Stadt und Christengemeinde zur Zeit des Paulus* (NovTSup 79; Leiden: Brill, 1995).

Collart, "Inscriptions"

> Paul Collart, "Inscriptions de Philippes," *BCH* 56 (1932) 192–231.

Collart, "Le sanctuaire des dieux égyptiens"

> Paul Collart, "Le sanctuaire des dieux égyptiens à Philippes," *BCH* 53 (1929) 70–100.

Collart, *Philippes*

Paul Collart, *Philippes, ville de Macédoine depuis ses origines jusqu'à la fin de l'époque romaine* (2 vols.; Paris: Boccard, 1937).

Collart and Ducrey, *Les reliefs rupestres*

Paul Collart and Pierre Ducrey, *Philippes I: Les reliefs rupestres* (BCH Sup. 2; Paris: École française d'Athènes, 1975).

Conzelmann, *Acts of the Apostles*

Hans Conzelmann, *The Acts of the Apostles* (Hermeneia; Philadelphia: Fortress, 1987).

Feissel, *Recueil des inscriptions*

D. Feissel, *Recueil des inscriptions chrétiennes de Macédoine du IIIe au VIe siècle* (BCH Sup. 8; Paris: École française d'Athènes, 1983).

Gounaris, *Balneum*

Georgios G. Gounaris, *The Balneum and the Northern Annexes of the Octagon of Philippi* (Athens: Library of the Archaeological Society of Athens 112, 1990) [in Greek].

Hammond, *History*

N. Hammond, *A History of Macedonia* (Oxford: Clarendon, 1959).

Hemer, *Book of Acts*

C. J. Hemer, *The Book of Acts in the Setting of Hellenistic History* (Winona Lake, Ind.: Eisenbrauns, 1990).

Heuzey and Daumet, *Mission archéologique*

L. Heuzey and H. Daumet, *Mission archéologique de Macédoine* (Paris: Librarie de Firmin-Didot et Cie, 1876).

Kajanto, *Supernomina*

Iiro Kajanto, *Supernomina: A Study in Latin Epigraphy* (Commentationes humanorum litterarum 40, no. 1; Helsinki, 1966).

Kavala and the Surrounding Area 1

Proceedings of the First Local Symposium on "Kavala and the Surrounding Area," Kavala 18–20 April 1977 (Thessalonike: Institute for Balkan Studies, 1980).

Kavala and the Surrounding Area 2

Proceedings of the Second Local Symposium on "Kavala and the Surrounding Area," Kavala 26–29 September 1986, Bulletin 1 (Kavala: Center for Historical Studies, 1987).

Kee, "The Transformation of the Synagogue"

Howard Clark Kee, "The Transformation of the Synagogue after 70 C.E.: Its Import for Early Christianity," *NTS* 36 (1990) 1–24.

Lazaridis, *Guide*

Demetrios Lazaridis, *Guide to the Kavala Museum* (Athens: D. Lazaridis, 1969) [in Greek].

Lazaridis, *Philippi*

Demetrios Lazaridis, *Philippi* (Thessalonike: D. Lazaridis, 1956) [in Greek].

Lazaridis, *Philippi: Roman Colony*

Demetrios Lazaridis, *Philippi: A Roman Colony* (Ancient Greek Cities 20; Athens: Athens Technological Organization and Athens Center of Ekistics, 1973) [in Greek].

Lemerle, *Philippes*

Paul Lemerle, *Philippes et la Macédoine orientale à l'époque chrétienne et byzantine* (Bibliothèque des Écoles Françaises d'Athènes et de Rome 158; Paris: Boccard, 1945).

MacDonald, *The Legend and the Apostle*

Dennis Ronald MacDonald, *The Legend and the Apostle* (Philadelphia: Westminster, 1983).

Memory to D. Lazaridis

Proceedings of the Archaeological Conference: Memory to D. Lazaridis: City and Country in Ancient Macedonia and Thrace, Kavala 9–11 May 1986 (Thessalonike: Recherches francohelléniques I, 1990).

Missitzis, "A Royal Decree"

L. Missitzis, "A Royal Decree of Alexander the Great on the Land of Philippi," *Ancient World* 12 (1985) 3–14.

Molisani, "GN. EGNATIUS"

G. Molisani, "GN. EGNATIUS C.F. e la data di costruzione della Via Egnazia," *Praktika tou VIII Diethnous Synedriou Ellenikis kai Latinikis Epigrafikis, Athens October 3rd–9th 1982* (Athens: Ministry of Culture and Science, 1984) 3. 108.

Nigdelis, "Synagogen"

P. M. Nigdelis, "Synagoge(n) und Gemeinde der Juden in Thessaloniki: Fragen aufgrund einer neuen jüdischen Grabinschrift der Kaiserzeit," *ZPE* 102 (1994) 297–306.

Papazoglou, "Le Territoire"

F. Papazoglou, "Le Territoire de la colonie de Philippes," *BCH* 106 (1982) 89–106.

Pelekanidis, "Conclusions from the Excavation of the Octagon"

Stylianos Pelekanidis, "Conclusions from the Excavation of the Octagon at Philippi Relating to the Monuments and Topography of the City," *Proceedings of the First Local Symposium on "Kavala and the Surrounding Area," Kavala 18–20 April 1977* (Thessalonike: Institute for Balkan Studies, 1980) 149–58 [in Greek].

Pelekanidis, "Kultprobleme im Apostel-Paulus Octogon."

Stylianos Pelekanidis, "Kultprobleme im Apostel-Paulus Octogon von Philippi im Zusammenhang mit einem älteren Heroenkult," *Atti del IX Congresso Internazionale di Archeologia Cristiana, Roma 21–27 Settembre 1975, II: Comunicazioni su scoperte inedite* (Studi di Antichità Cristiana 32, 2 vols.; Vatican City: Pontificio Istituto di Archeologia Cristiana, 1978) 2. 393–97.

Pelekanidis, "Philippi"

Stylianos Pelekanidis, "Philippi and Its Christian Monuments," in *Celebration of the Fortieth Anniversary of the Society for Macedonian Studies* (Thessalonike: Society for Macedonian Studies, 1980) 101–25 [in Greek].

Pelekanidis, *Studien*

Stylianos Pelekanidis, "The Extramural Early Christian Basilica of Philippi," *Studien zur frühchristlichen und byzantinischen Archäologie* (Thessalonike: Institute for Balkan Studies, 1977) 333–94] [in Greek].

Pelekanidou and Mentzos, "The Octagon"

Elli Pelekanidou and Aristoteles Mentzos, "The Octagon of Philippi: Initial Conclusions Following Recent Investigations," *Memory to D. Lazaridis, 597–606* [in Greek].

Reynolds and Tannenbaum, *Jews and Godfearers at Aphrodisias*

Joyce Maire Reynolds and Robert Tannenbaum, *Jews and Godfearers at Aphrodisias: Greek Inscriptions with Commentary Text from the Excavations at Aphrodisias Conducted by K. T. Erim* (Sup. vol. 12; Cambridge: Cambridge Philological Society, 1987).

Robert, "Inscriptions juives"

Louis Robert, "Inscriptions juives," *Hellenica* 11–12 (1960).

Robinson, *Nag Hammadi*

James M. Robinson, ed., *The Nag Hammadi Library in English* (4th rev. ed.; Leiden: Brill, 1998).

Roger, "L'enceinte basse de Philippes"

Jacques Roger, "L'enceinte basse de Philippes," *BCH* 62 (1938) 21–41.

Rolley, "Les cultes égyptiens"

C. Rolley, "Les cultes égyptiens à Thasos: à propos de quelques documents nouveaux," *BCH* 112 (1968) 187–219.

Romiopoulou, "Un nouveau milliaire"

K. Romiopoulou, "Un nouveau milliaire de la Via Egnatia," *BCH* 98 (1974) 813–18.

Salomies, *Die römischen Vornamen*

O. Salomies, *Die römischen Vornamen: Studien zur römischen Namengebung* (Commentationes Humanorum Litterarum 82; Helsinki: Societas Scientiarum Fennica, 1987).

Samartzidou, "Via Egnatia"

Stavroula Samartzidou, "The Via Egnatia: From Philippi to Neapolis," *Memory to D. Lazaridis,* 559–87 [in Greek].

Schneemelcher, *New Testament Apocrypha*

Wilhelm Schneemelcher, ed., *The New Testament Apocrypha* (rev. ed. of Edgar Hennecke's collection; trans. R. McL. Wilson et al.; 2 vols.; Philadelphia: Westminster/John Knox, 1991).

Sève and Weber, "Un monument honorifique"

M. Sève and P. Weber, "Un monument honorifique au forum de Philippes," *BCH* 112 (1988) 467–79.

Tataki, *Ancient Beroea*

A. Tataki, *Ancient Beroea: Prosopography and Society* (Athens: Centre for Greek and Roman Antiquity, National Hellenic Research Foundation, 1988).

Touratsoglou and Rizakis, *Inscriptions*

I. Touratsoglou and A. Rizakis, *Inscriptions from Upper Macedonia* (Athens: Ministry of Culture, 1985).

Trebilco, *Jewish Communities in Asia Minor*

P. Trebilco, *Jewish Communities in Asia Minor* (Cambridge: Cambridge University Press, 1991).

Vatin, "Lettre adressée à la cité de Philippes"

Claude Vatin, "Lettre adressée à la cité de Philippes par les ambassadeurs auprès d' Alexandre," *Praktika tou VIII Diethnous Synedriou Ellenikis kai Latinikis Epigrafikis, Athens October 3rd–9th 1982* (Athens: Ministry of Culture and Science, 1984) 1. 259–70.

Introduction

Almost twenty years ago, in May of 1979, the first of a series of Harvard University seminars on "Archaeology and the World of the New Testament" visited Philippi in Macedonia. At that time, the two editors of this volume began the long process of developing a discourse between the disciplines of New Testament studies and archaeological explorations. Over the years, it became clear that only a joint effort would bring us closer to solving puzzling problems that beset both the understanding of early Christian texts relating to Philippi and the interpretation of the recent excavations at this ancient Macedonian city and, in particular, of the Octagonal Church complex. The result of our discussions was the plan to organize a small "Symposium on Paul and Philippi."

This symposium took place in May 1993 in Kavala, the ancient Neapolis, in the Ephoreia of Byzantine Antiquities. Several dozen invited guests from Kavala, Thessalonike, Athens, Cyprus, and the United States participated, including the Harvard students who were members of that year's seminar "Archaeology and the World of the New Testament." The bishop of Neapolis and Philippi, who gave an introductory speech on the history of the episcopacy during the apostolic period, later invited participants to a generous lunch in the entrance building to the chapel of Lydia in Philippi. A visit to the site of the Octagonal Church excavations followed.

The four papers presented at this symposium form the content of this book. There were two concerns that inspired our investigation. First of all, rather than discussing ancient Philippi in general, we wanted to forge a better understanding of the development of the city over the centuries and the chronology of its archaeological evidence in order to distinguish more clearly between the Hellenistic, early Roman, and the subsequent early Christian periods. This, we hope, has been achieved in the first two essays of this book. The essay of Chaido Koukouli-Chrysantaki, ephorus of Classical Antiquities of Eastern Macedonia and director of the Archaeological Museum in Kavala, will guide the reader to a much clearer understanding of the Roman colony of Philippi at the time of the apostle Paul's visit and in the second century CE. Included in the essay is the first publication of a newly discovered inscription from the very end of that period, which gives evidence for the existence of a Jewish synagogue. The contribution of Charalambos Bakirtzis, professor at the Aristotle University of Thessalonike and ephorus of Byzantine Antiquities of Central Macedonia in Thessalonike (at the time of the symposium, ephorus of Byzantine Antiquities of Eastern Macedonia and Thrace in Kavala), presents the first comprehensive account of the excavations of the Octagonal Church complex and its development from the beginnings in the early fourth century — the earliest datable Christian assembly hall in all of Greece and Macedonia — to its final destruction at the end of the early Christian period in the beginning of the seventh century CE, which marks the end of antiquity and the loss of technology.

Our second concern was to juxtapose the interpretation of the archaeological evidence with a most thorough critical reading of early Christian literary evidence. This is attempted in the essays of Helmut Koester and Allen Callahan, both professors of New Testament studies at Harvard Divinity School. We were aware of the fact that the archaeological evidence suggested that, in the fourth and later centuries,

Philippi must have been a center of pilgrimage honoring Paul's martyrdom. Therefore our search was for earlier literary evidence for a tradition of Paul's martyrdom in Philippi rather than in Rome, noting that the latter tradition is not attested anywhere before the end of the second century CE. It should be noted that we are not arguing for the historical fact of a martyrdom of Paul in the East. All traditions of the martyrdom of the apostles of the first generation are legendary. The Christians of the earliest period were not interested in hero worship and in fixing and localizing the places of the deaths and burials of the apostles. Later establishments and rituals devoted to the memory of early apostles, however, may indeed preserve earlier traditions that have left their traces in some of the extant Christian literature. Our essays argue that attestation in early Christian literature for Philippi as the place of Paul's martyrdom is strong and seems to be supported by the later archaeological record, while Rome's claim to that honor lacks early literary attestation.

Whether or not readers find the hypotheses of these essays persuasive, we hope that the challenge to interpret critically both the archaeological and the literary evidence and to establish some correlation between them will be a fruitful basis for further discussion. The discourse between New Testament scholars and archaeologists needs to be cultivated and refined. The use of archaeological evidence for the verification of the historicity of biblical reports has to become a thing of the past. Archaeology can no longer be employed to support traditional assumptions about the historicity of early Christian literary information, whether this be the question of Peter in Rome or of Paul in Philippi. However, the combined effort of archaeologists and of scholars of the history of early Christianity may lead to a better understanding of the development of religious traditions and rituals, in which the memory of the past was alive in early Christian communities.

For excellent assistance in the preparation of the manuscript, the editors are grateful to Elizabeth Lerner, alumna of Harvard Divinity School, and Mark Kurtz, currently enrolled in the Ph.D. program in the Study of Religion at Harvard University. Mark Kurtz also gave invaluable assistance in the proofreading and in guiding this book through the stages of its production, devoting faithfully his time, energies, and expert knowledge and untiring care to this publication. Finally, Laura Nasrallah, student in the Th.D. program at Harvard Divinity School, assisted in the correcting of the proofs. All three helpful assistants have been members of the seminar Archaeology and the World of the New Testament.

CHARALAMBOS BAKIRTZIS

HELMUT KOESTER

Cambridge, Mass., and Thessaloniki
October 1998

1

COLONIA IULIA AUGUSTA PHILIPPENSIS

Chaido Koukouli-Chrysantaki

Introduction

The original name of the Greek city of Philippi was Krenides, which means a site "with many springs."[1] Krenides was the Thasians' last colony in ancient Thrace, founded in 360 BCE, probably on the site of an older city named Datos (fig. 1).[2]

---

1. Appian *BCiv.* 4.105: "Philippi is a city that was formerly called Datos, and before that Krenides, because there are many springs bubbling around a hill there" (οἱ δὲ Φίλιπποι πόλις ἐστί, ἢ Δάτος ὠνομάζετο πάλαι καὶ Κρηνίδες ἔτι πρὸ Δάτου. Κρῆναι γάρ εἰσι περὶ τῷ λόφῳ ναμάτων πολλαί).
2. Harpocration on Datos: "The city of the Dateni was renamed when Philipp, the king of the Macedonians, seized it" (μετωνομάσθη μέντοι ἡ πόλις τῶν Δατηνῶν, Φιλίππου τοῦ Μακεδόνων βασιλέως κρατήσαντος αὐτῆς, Harpocration, *Lexicon* [Lipsiae: Hartmann, 1824] 45–46). Scylax 67: Νεάπολις κατὰ ταύτην Δάτον, πόλις ἑλληνὶς ἦν ᾤκισεν Καλλίστρατος αὐτῆς (C. Müller, *GGM* I, 54). See also: "Datos of the good things, the name of the city, which the Thasians colonized" (Δάτος ἀγαθῶν, ὄνομα πόλεως συνῴκισεν Θάσιοι; *Corpus Paroemiographorum Graecorum* [Göttingen: 1839–52] 1. 60). Eustathius in Dionysius Periegeta 517: "And Thasos, which also had gold, once also inhabited Datos, a famous city along the seaboard of the Strymon" (καὶ Θάσος, ἥτις καὶ χρυσία εἶχε, ποτὲ καὶ τὸ Δάτον συνῴκισεν, πόλιν ἔνδοξον περὶ τὴν τοῦ Στρυμόνος παραλίαν, C. Müller, *GGM* I). See also Heuzey and Daumet, *Mission archéologique*, 1–67; Collart, *Philippes*, 1. 133–60; Fanoula Papazoglou,

The Thasian colony occupied a very privileged site on a major road connecting the Aegean coast with the Thracian hinterland. It also held a fertile plain, surrounded by mountains that were rich in gold and silver.[3] With the founding of this Thasian colony, coins (including the first gold ones) were minted bearing the legend ΘΑΣΙΟΝ ΗΠΕΙΡΟ (pl. I,1). It was precisely because of its privileged situation that Krenides enjoyed only a short period as an independent Thasian colony.

In 356 BCE, the Thasian colonists of Krenides invited Philipp II of Macedonia to help them fight the local Thracian tribes.[4] Philipp had been intending to extend the frontiers of his kingdom to east of the Strymon,[5] and realizing the im-

---

Les villes de Macédoine à l'époque romaine (BCH Sup. 16; Athens: École française d'Athènes, 1988) 405–13; François Salviat, "La Lettre XI de Platon: Léodamas de Thasos, Kallistratos d'Athènes et la fondation de Krénides," *Études Classiques, II, Annales de la Faculté des Lettres et Sciences Humaines d'Aix* 43 (1967) 43–56; Vatin, "Lettre adressée à la cité de Philippes," 259–70; Missitzis, "A Royal Decree," 12–13; Oliver Picard, "Les Thasiens du continent et la fondation de Philippes," *Tranquillitas, Mélanges en l'honneur de Tran Tam Tihn* (Quebec: Collection: Hier Pour Aujourd'hui, 1944) 459–74.

3. The colony of Krenides was situated between Mount Pangaion and the Orbelos (Lekani) Range, where ancient gold and silver mines have been located. Strabo 7, fr. 34: "There are very many gold mines in Krenides, where now the city Philippi is situated, near Mount Pangaion" (ὅτι πλεῖστα μέταλλά ἐστι χρυσοῦ ἐν ταῖς Κρηνίσιν, ὅπου νῦν οἱ Φίλιπποι πόλις ἵδρυται, πλησίον τοῦ Παγγαίου ὄρους); see Chaido Koukouli-Chrysantaki, "The Metals of the Thasian Mainland," *Memory to D. Lazaridis,* 493–532 [in Greek].

4. Stephanus Byzantius on Philippi: "...and the city Philippi, formerly Krenides. The Krenidians were warring with the Thracians. Because of Philipp's helping, they named it for Philipp" (καὶ πόλις Φίλιπποι τὸ παλαιὸν Κρηνίδες. τοῖς δὲ Κρηνίταις πολεμουμένοις ὑπὸ Θρακῶν βοηθήσας ὁ Φίλιππος Φιλίππους ὠνόμασεν). Collart, *Philippes,* 1. 152–60; Hammond, *History,* 251, 255.

5. He captured Amphipolis in 358 BCE (Hammond, *History,* 230–37).

portance of the site, he conquered the city, fortified it with new walls, and renamed it Philippi.[6] He also intensified the exploitation of the local gold and silver mines,[7] increased the city's population, and transformed Philippi into a stronghold of the Macedonian kingdom. He struck his first gold coins in local gold,[8] but allowed the city to continue producing its own coinage (pl. I,2).[9]

Philippi flourished during the reigns of Philipp II and Alexander the Great,[10] but little is known about its history in the

---

6. Diodorus Siculus 16.3.7: "While these things were going on, the Thasians settled the place called Krenides, which the king later named Philippi for himself and made a populous settlement" (ἅμα δὲ τούτοις πραττομένοις Θάσιοι μὲν ὤκισαν τὰς ὀνομαζομένας Κρηνίδας, ἃς ὕστερον ὁ βασιλεὺς ἀφ᾽ ἑαυτοῦ ὀνομάσας Φιλίππους ἐπλήρωσεν οἰκητόρων). Harpocration: "Datos, of course the city of the Datians, was named after Philipp, king of Macedon who held it" (Δατός, μετωνομάσθη μέντοι ἡ πόλις τῶν Δατηνῶν Φιλίππου τῶν Μακεδόνων βασιλέως κρατήσαντος αὐτῆς). Appian, *BCiv.* 4.105: "Philip fortified it because he considered it an excellent stronghold against the Thracians, and named it for himself, Philippi" (Φίλιππος δὲ ὡς εὐφυὲς ἐπὶ Θράκης χωρίον ὠχύρωσέ τε καὶ ἀφ᾽ ἑαυτοῦ Φιλίππους προσεῖπεν).

7. Diodorus Siculus 16.8.6–7: "Turning to the gold mines in its territory which were very scanty and insignificant, he increased their output so much by his improvements that they could bring him a revenue of more than a thousand talents" (Τὰ δὲ κατὰ τὴν χώραν χρύσεια μέταλλα παντελῶς ὄντα λιτὰ καὶ ἄδοξα ταῖς κατασκευαῖς ἐπὶ τοσοῦτον ηὔξησεν ὥστε δύνασθαι φέρειν αὐτῷ πρόσοδον πλεῖον ταλάντων χιλίων).

8. Diodorus Siculus 16.8.7: "For with the gold coins which he struck, which came to be known from his name as Philippeioi, he organized a large force of mercenaries, and by using these coins for bribes induced many Greeks to become betrayers of their native lands" (νόμισμα γὰρ χρυσοῦν κόψας τὸ προσαγορευθὲν ἀπ᾽ ἐκείνου Φιλίππειον μισθοφόρων τε δύναμιν ἀξιόλογον συνεστήσατο καὶ τῶν Ἑλλήνων πολλοὺς διὰ τούτου προετρέψατο προδότας γενέσθαι τῶν πατρίδων). G. le Rider, *Le Monnayage d'argent et d'or de Philippe II* (Paris: Bourgey, 1977).

9. A. R. Bellintzer, "Philippi in Macedonia," *ANSMN* 11 (1964) 29–52.

10. Vatin, "Lettre adressée à la cité de Philippes," 259–70; Missitzis, "A Royal Decree," 3–14.

Hellenistic period.[11] The second chapter in the city's history opened after the Romans occupied Macedonia in 148 BCE. The construction of the Via Egnatia,[12] which ran through Philippi, was a new landmark in its history. It was, however, the Battle of Philippi in 42 BCE that truly brought the city into the historical limelight.[13] The battle was fought outside the west wall (the landscape described by Appian remains unchanged to this day),[14] and the victors, Antony and Octavian, settled the first Roman veterans there and founded the first Roman colony. It was Antony who struck the new colony's first coins (pl. I,3a–b).[15] Later, after the Battle of Actium in 31 BCE, Octavian brought more Roman veterans and colonists and installed them in Philippi and its fertile surroundings. The city rapidly developed into a flourishing Roman colony under the name of "Colonia Augusta Iulia Philippensis" (pl. I,4a–b).[16] A new Roman aristocracy was

---

11. G. Klaffenbach, "Asylienurkunden aus Kos," *Abhandlungen der Akademie Berlin 1952, 15* (Berlin: Akademie-Verlag, 1952) = *SEG* 12 (1955) no. 373; C. Schuler, "The Macedonian Politarchs," *CP* 55 (1960) 90.

12. Romiopoulou, "Un nouveau milliaire," 813–16; Molisani, "GN. EGNATIUS."

13. Appian *BCiv.* 4.105–38; Dio Cassius *Hist. Rom.* 47.35–49; Plutarch *Vit. Brut.* 38–53; *Vit. Ant.* 22. See also Strabo *Geogr.* 7, fr. 41: "In earlier times Philippi was called Krenides, and was only a small settlement, but it was enlarged after the defeat of Brutus and Cassius" (Οἱ δὲ Φίλιπποι Κρηνίδες ἐκαλοῦντο πρότερον, κατοικία μικρά, ηὐξήθη δὲ μετὰ τὴν περὶ Βροῦτον καὶ Κάσσιον ἧτταν).

14. Heuzey and Daumet, *Mission archéologique,* 97–116; Collart, *Philippes,* 1. 191–219.

15. See H. Gaebler, "Die erste koloniale Prägung in Philippi," *Zeitschrift für Numismatik* 39 (1929) 260–69; Collart, *Philippes,* 1. 224–47.

16. It was called "Colonia Iulia Philippensis" in 30 BCE and became "Colonia Augusta Iulia Philippensis" or "Colonia Iulia Augusta Philippensis" after 16 January 27 BCE; cf. Collart, *Philippes,* 1. 228–37.

established in this Macedonian city, new coins were minted, and new buildings constructed.[17] Roman power was consolidated when Claudius conquered Thrace and made it a province of the Roman Empire in 44 CE.[18] It was to this flourishing city of the Julio-Claudian period that Paul came in 49 or 50 CE.

The arrival of Paul and the foundation of the first Christian church began the third major chapter in the history of Philippi. The Acts of the Apostles (Acts 16:11) recounts the journey of Saint Paul and his companions Silas, Timothy, and Luke from Asia Minor to Samothrake and the port of Neapolis.

Neapolis was another Thasian colony founded on the mainland opposite Thasos (fig. 1). In the seventh century BCE it flourished as a city-state; it was then independent of the island of Thasos from the end of the sixth to the middle of the fourth century BCE, when it was incorporated into the Macedonian kingdom. As Philippi developed, Neapolis declined until it became Philippi's port.[19] Nothing now remains of Neapolis, which lay farther inland than the modern port,[20] apart from a bollard of Thessalian marble[21] and some busts atop marble pilasters, which attest to a city of monumental

17. For the coins of Augustus in Philippi, see Collart, *Philippes*, 1. 235–37, pl. 30.5.7; for the monuments, see Collart, *Philippes*, 1. 318–88.

18. Coins were minted in Philippi during the reign of Claudius; H. Gaebler, *Die antiken Münzen von Macedonia und Päonia*, Abt. 2 (Berlin: de Gruyter, 1935) 103, pl. 20.16

19. Bakalakis, "Neapolis, Christoupolis, Kavala," 1–2; Lazaridis, *Guide*, 13.

20. Bakalakis, "Neapolis, Christoupolis, Kavala," fig. 2.

21. There is no clear evidence for its dating. The Thessalian provenance of the marble points to the early Christian period.

buildings in the Roman period.[22] Stone sarcophagi found in the modern city of Kavala (ancient Neapolis) bear witness to the eminent Roman citizens of Colonia Iulia Philippensis who lived and died in its port of Neapolis. One of these, who may have lived in Saint Paul's time, was Cornelia Asprilla, a priestess of Livia Augusta.[23]

Its connection with Saint Paul's first steps in Europe gave Neapolis a distinguished place in the new Christian world. Architectural fragments built into Kavala's medieval fortress and early Ottoman buildings attest the existence of early Christian buildings in Neapolis.[24] A fragment of an ambo with relief decoration[25] is evidence for a monumental early Christian church in Neapolis. The city later changed its name to Christoupolis.[26]

---

22. Kavala Museum Inv. no. Λ289–293. A hoard of coins from the third century CE has been found on the same site (Kavala Museum Inv. no. M126). Neapolis was an important station on the Via Egnatia: see P. Collart, "Une réfection de la Via Egnatia sous Trajan," *BCH* 59 (1935) 407–8; in a milliary of Thessalonike we read: "USQUE NEAPOLI(M)." See also a milliary of Septimius Severus found in the modern city of Kavala: A. Salac, "Inscriptions du Pangée, de la région Drama-Cavalla et de Philippes," *BCH* 47 (1923) 80.

23. Heuzey and Daumet, *Mission archéologique,* 15–21, nos. 1–4; Kavala Museum Inv. no. Λ275.

24. Bakalakis, "Neapolis, Christoupolis, Kavala," 48; Lazaridis, *Guide,* 26; X. Pennas, *Kavala,* in "Macedonia-Thrace," *ADelt* 32B (1977) 264 [in Greek]; E. Kourkoutidou-Nikolaodou, *Kavala,* in "Macedonia-Thrace," *ADelt* 33B (1978) 322–23 [in Greek].

25. H. Maguire, "An Early Christian Marble Relief at Kavala," *Deltion tis Christianikis Archeologikis Etaireias* 4th period, 16 (1991/92) 283–95.

26. Bakalakis, "Neapolis, Christoupolis, Kavala," 47; idem, "The Wall at Christoupolis," *Ellinika* 10 (1938) 307–18 [in Greek]; K. Chionis, *History of Kavala* (Kavala, 1968) [in Greek]; Lazaridis, *Guide,* 27–42; Charalambos Bakirtzis, *Kavala,* in "Macedonia-Thrace," *ADelt* 32B (1977) 264; 33B (1978) 323–24; 41B (1986) 175–76 [in Greek].

From Neapolis to Philippi

According to the Acts of the Apostles,[27] Saint Paul and his companions did not stay in Neapolis. They continued their journey, along the Via Egnatia, to Philippi. One can follow the course of the road easily; the stone-paved road on the hill of the modern Monastery of Saint Silas was the successor to the Via Egnatia (pl. I,5).[28]

Recent investigations[29] have produced further evidence; near the village of Amygdaleonas, at a site named Vassilaki at the foot of a hill crowned with an ancient fortified akropolis, a *mansio* of the Via Egnatia has been found. Archaeological and literary evidence shows that this station continued to be used throughout the Byzantine and into the post-Byzantine period.[30] Stavroula Samartzidou has proposed that the site be identified as the *Fons CO* in the *Tabula Peutigeriana*.[31] Paul and his companions may well have stopped at this very station, midway between Neapolis and Philippi, to rest and drink water from a well like the one that survives there today (pl. II,1).

From *Fons CO* the Via Egnatia continued westward to Philippi (fig. 2). Samartzidou describes some of the archaeological data relating to the Via Egnatia. Excavations in Amygdaleonas have yielded part of the road itself and a

---

27. Acts 16:12; Hemer, *Book of Acts*, 115, 116 n. 30.
28. Lazaridis, *Guide*, 26.
29. Samartzidou, "Via Egnatia," 559–87 [in Greek].
30. Vassilaki has been correctly identified as the Byzantine village where the magister Basilakios was blinded by Emperor Nikephoros Botaniates; see K. Orfanidis, "The Magister Basilacius and the Site of Vassilaki," *Pavlios Etairia Meleton* 3 (1978) 25–26 [in Greek]; Samartzidou, "Via Egnatia," 572.
31. *Tabula Peutigeriana*, col. VII; Samartzidou, "Via Egnatia," 573–75.

milliary.[32] The road was paved with stone, and the milliary (pl. II,2) bears a bilingual text containing the name of the proconsul Gnaeus Egnatius, who constructed the Via Egnatia.[33] This milliary and another one with a similar text found near Thessalonike[34] are the oldest milliaries on the Via Egnatia and date to the original construction of the road in the second half of the second century BCE. St. Paul might have passed them both on his way from Neapolis to Philippi and thence to Thessalonike.

West of the modern Amygdaleonas (fig. 2) the Via Egnatia continued through the local marshes towards Philippi.[35] Just before the city walls the apostle arrived at another spring, where the monument to the Roman legionary C. Vibius Quartus was later erected (pl. III,1).[36] Some scholars propose that this site, which is known as Dikili Tas or Megalo Lithari,[37] was the location of the *Fons CO* of the *Tabula Peutigeriana*.[38] I am more convinced by Samartzidou's theory that the *mansio* was located midway between Neapolis and Philippi, rather than closer to the latter.[39] The need for a station with a khan here, so near the city, did not arise until much later, in the Ottoman period, when Philippi was deserted.[40]

---

32. Samartzidou, "Via Egnatia," 559–64, figs. 1–6.
33. Molisani, "GN. EGNATIUS," 108.
34. Romiopoulou, "Un nouveau milliaire," 816–18.
35. Samartzidou, "Via Egnatia," 568–69.
36. Heuzey and Daumet, *Mission archéologique*, 45, nos. 21–22; Collart, *Philippes*, 1. 326; Samartzidou, "Via Egnatia," 568–69. Concerning C. Vibius Quartus, see also G. A. Souris, "New Latin Inscriptions from Macedonia" (paper presented at the Third International Conference on Macedonia ["Inscriptions from Macedonia"], Aristotle University of Thessalonike, 8–12 December 1993; in press [in Greek]).
37. Heuzey and Daumet, *Mission archéologique*, 43.
38. Ibid.; Collart, *Philippes*, 1. 497–98.
39. Samartzidou, "Via Egnatia," 564–65.
40. Heuzey and Daumet, *Mission archéologique*, pl. 1.

As he made his way along the Via Egnatia, Paul must have passed this spring and possibly a sanctuary of the mother goddess Cybele near the road.[41] Passing the Roman city's east cemetery,[42] he would have entered Philippi by the east gate, the "Neapolis Gate," as the French excavators dubbed it (pl. III,2 and fig. 3,1a).[43]

Philippi

The City

When Paul arrived, the gate must still have had its original form. The niche at the entrance, which must have contained a cult relief, is reminiscent of the niches of the gods who protected the gates in the walls of metropolitan Thasos.[44] So Paul would have entered the city under the eye of its propylaean god, who was later joined by Isis Regina.[45] In time, the altar of Isis received Christian symbols, and Christian Philippi eventually protected its main gate with the text of the letter from Christ to Abgar.[46]

---

41. Ibid., 43, no. 19; Collart, *Philippes,* 1. 326.

42. Heuzey and Daumet, *Mission archéologique,* 44–48; Collart, *Philippes,* 1. 325–26.

43. Roger, "L'enceinte basse de Philippes," 26–30.

44. Ch. Picard, "Les Murailles: Les portes sculptées à images divines," Études Thasiennes 8 (1962) 47, fig. 15; 89, fig. 35; 114, fig. 47; 115, fig. 53; 151, fig. 66.

45. Collart, "Le sanctuaire des dieux égyptiens," 70–100.

46. The symbols (a cross and a bird) incised on the pagan altar and the inscription of the text of Christ's letter built into the wall by the Neapolis Gate were a continuation of the tradition of protecting the entrance to the city. Ch. Picard, "Un texte nouveau de la correspondance entre Abgar d'Osroène et Jésus Christ gravé sur une porte de ville à Philippes (Macédoine)," BCH 44 (1920) 41–46. See also idem, "Les dieux de la colonie de Philippes," RHR 86 (1922) 183. Another (fragmentary) inscrip-

We know very little about Julio-Claudian Philippi in the middle of the first century CE when Paul and his companions arrived there. But the ἥτις ἐστιν πρώτης μερίδος τῆς Μακεδονίας πόλις κολωνεία[47] ("a city which belongs to the first district of Macedonia, a [Roman] colony") must have developed along the lines of the Macedonian city's original plan (pl. V).[48]

Excavations have found Hellenistic streets under the Roman ones in the area of the Octagon[49] and to the north of the Via Egnatia (pl. VI,1).[50] By the time Paul arrived, however, the new building programs implemented by Augustus and Claudius already must have changed much of the Macedonian city.[51] The Julio-Claudian city was in turn con-

---

tion calling upon Christ to protect the city was also found at the Neapolis Gate; cf. Collart, *Philippes,* 1. 468 n. 1; Lemerle, *Philippes,* 90–91.

47. Lemerle, *Philippes,* 19–23; Hemer, *Book of Acts,* 113–14 n. 31.

48. The plan of Philippi shares many similarities with those of the cities in the Near East founded by the Macedonian kings who succeeded Alexander the Great; see J. C. Balty, "L'urbanisme de la Tetrapolis syrienne," *International Meeting of History and Archeology: O Ellinismos stin Anatoli, Delphi 6–9 November 1986* (Athens: European Cultural Center at Delphi, 1991) 216, fig. 7 (Laodicea). For the moment, however, it is impossible to recognize the remains of the earlier Thasian colony of Krenides in the existing archaeological evidence.

49. Pelekanidis, "Philippi," 113–25; G. Lavas, "The Cities of the 'Christian Basilicas': A Contribution to the Urban Planning of Eastern Illyricum," *Actes du Xe Congrès International d'Archéologie Chrétienne,* 592.

50. *ADelt* 45B (1990) 386–89.

51. The first phase of the forum is not accurately dated. However, the first forum must have been planned from the very beginning of the Roman colony; cf. Collart, *Philippes,* 1. 357 n. 2; M. Sève, "Travaux de l'École française en Gréce en 1984: Philippes," *BCH* 109 (1985) 870. We do not know the location of the agora of Macedonian Philippi; however, traces of Hellenistic buildings have been found under the stone pavement of the central court of the forum: Chaido Koukouli, *Kavala,* in "Antiquities and Monuments of Eastern Macedonia," *ADelt* 23 B2 (1968) 352, pl. 299e [in Greek].

siderably changed by later building phases, so very few of the buildings from Paul's time can be traced under the monumental edifices constructed by Antoninus Pius and later by Justinian (pl. IV).

From the Neapolis Gate, the Via Egnatia[52] traversed the center of Philippi, probably as a *decumanus,* and passed along the north side of the forum (pl. V,18). We do not know precisely when Philippi's first forum was built; however, it certainly existed when Paul arrived. Excavations have revealed remains of it under the Antonine forum (pl. V,9).[53] The remains have been identified under the buildings along the east, west, and north sides of the second forum.

The general plan of the earlier forum coincides with that of the Antonine forum. The former had a larger central square, but the two temple-shaped structures on the north side must have served the same purpose as their counterparts in the latter. The structure at the west end of the Antonine forum has been recognized as the *curia* of the Roman colony.[54] The temple at the east end must have been devoted

---

52. The name is purely conventional. The street is the city's *decumanus maximus,* the shortest route between the east gate (Neapolis) and the west gate. The so-called Commercial Road was more convenient for chariots. For the Via Egnatia in Philippi, see Collart, *Philippes,* 1. 487; Lazaridis, *Philippi: Roman Colony,* 41; Pelekanidis, "Philippi," 105–6; M. Sève and P. Weber, "Philippi," *BCH* 106 (1982) Chronique, 651; G. Gounaris and G. Velenis, "Philippi Excavation 1991," *To Archaeologiko Ergo sti Makedonia kai Thraki* 5 (1991) (Thessalonike: Ministry of Culture, Ministry of Macedonia and Thrace, Aristotle University of Thessalonike, 1994) 406–17, fig. 1 [in Greek].

53. Collart, *Philippes,* 1. 350–58; M. Sève, "Un décret de consolation à Cyzique," *BCH* 103 (1979) 327–59; Chronique, 627–31, fig. 16; *BCH* 104 (1980) Chronique, 712–16, fig. 31; *BCH* 105 (1981) Chronique, 918–23, fig. 1; *BCH* 109 (1985) Chronique, 870.

54. Sève and Weber, "Philippi," 651, fig. 1.

to the emperors' cult.[55] The cult of Augustus,[56] as also of his adopted sons Gaius and Lucius Caesar (pl. VI, 2),[57] already existed in Philippi when Paul arrived. The cult of Livia had been introduced by Claudius in 44 CE,[58] but the apostle may not have seen the monument with the statues of the seven priestesses in front of the temple, because it was probably not built until the second half of the first century CE.[59]

As a Roman citizen, Paul must have strolled in the forum, where statues of Augustus and his family stood,[60] together with monuments to the Julio-Claudian emperors, eminent citizens of the Colonia Augusta Iulia Philippensis,[61] and the local Thracian kings.[62] It was in the forum too that Paul faced the magistrates (στρατηγοί),[63] prob-

---

55. Ibid., 651; Sève and Weber, "Un monument honorifique," 479.

56. Collart, *Philippes*, 1. 412.

57. The cult of Augustus's adopted sons Gaius and Lucius is well attested on Thasos: F. Chamoux, "Un portrait de Thasos: Lucius César," *Monuments et Memoires: Fondation E. Piot* 4 (1950) 92–96.

58. G. Grether, "Livia and the Roman Imperial Cult," *AJP* 47 (1946) 222–52; W. Kiedorf, " 'Funus' und 'consecratio': Zu Terminologie und Ablauf der römischen Kaiserapotheose," *Chiron, Mitteilungen der Kommission für Alte Geschichte und Epigraphik des Deutschen Archäologischen Instituts* 16 (1986) 61. The cult of Livia was popular until the second century CE.

59. Sève and Weber, "Un monument honorifique," 467–79.

60. Portrait of Augustus (?) or Gaius Caesar (?); cf. Collart, *Philippes*, 1. 353, pl. LXXXIII, 4; Philippi Museum Inv. no. Λ31. Portrait of Gaius Caesar (?); cf. W. H. Gross, "Zweimal Gaius," *Archäologischer Anzeiger* 86 (1971) 562. The portrait (pl. VI, 2) reminds one also of portraits of Germanicus.

61. M. Lolius, in Collart, "Inscriptions," 206, fig. 10; Collart, *Philippes*, 1. 248, 353.

62. Roemitalces, in Collart, "Inscriptions," 20, no. 4, fig. 9; Collart, *Philippes*, 1. 253, 353.

63. Acts 16:19–21. For a discussion and bibliography concerning the Latin equivalents of the Greek titles ἄρχοντες and στρατηγοί, see Lemerle, *Philippes*, 32 n. 4 and 33 n. 2. Lemerle proposes the general term "authorities" and recognizes the colonial magistrates, the *duoviri*, in the latter.

ably in one of the administrative buildings on the west side.[64]

During his short visit to Philippi, Paul may also have walked along the street at the south end of the forum, the so-called Commercial Road (pl. V,10).[65] Its present excavated form dates to the early Christian period, but the road itself is much older, for it was part of the original plan of the Macedonian city. It was certainly serving its commercial function in Paul's time.

We know nothing about the Roman city farther south of the forum at the time of Paul's visit. Excavators date the Roman buildings, the commercial agora,[66] and the palaestra[67] discovered under the early Christian Basilica B[68] to a much later date in the second century CE. Nor do we have a clear picture of that part of Philippi that lay to the north of the Via Egnatia (and the modern road). This was in fact the nucleus of the Greek city, and archaeological evidence shows it to have been the city's religious center. That it was a cult center is attested by the existence of the second-century CE rock sanctuaries and by the cult's continuation into the early Christian period. The area was radically changed, however, by Antonine, and later Justinian, building programs.

Hemer, *Book of Acts,* 115 n. 34, interprets ἄρχοντες as a general term and στρατηγοί as *duoviri.*

64. Collart, *Philippes,* 1. 339–40; Sève and Weber, "Philippi," 651–53, fig. 1.

65. Collart, *Philippes,* 1. 364; Lazaridis, *Philippi: Roman Colony,* 33; Gounaris and Velenis, "Philippi Excavation 1991," 409–17; Stylianos Pelekanidis, "Excavation of Philippi," *Praktika Archaeologikis Etaireias* (Athens) 1976, 115–17 [in Greek]; idem, "Philippi," 104–5; idem, "Conclusions from the Excavation of the Octagon," 151–52.

66. J. Coupry, "Un joueur de marelle au marché de Philippes," *BCH* 70 (1946) 103, fig. 1.

67. P. Lemerle, "Palestre romaine à Philippes," *BCH* 61 (1937) 86–102, fig. 1, pl. IX.

68. Lemerle, *Philippes,* 429–513.

In the area north of the Via Egnatia stood one of the city's most important public buildings, the theater,[69] which was built at the same time as the city walls and certainly dates to the very foundation of the Greek city (pl. VII,1). At the time of Paul's visit, the theater must still have retained much of its original fourth-century BCE form. Little of the original structure was preserved during its successive restorations and transformations. To the west of the theater are sanctuaries on the slopes of the akropolis that date from after Paul's time. The rock sanctuaries[70] and the Sanctuary of the Egyptian Gods[71] date to the second century CE, but the existence of earlier cult centers in this area cannot be ruled out. The Sanctuary of Dionysos, for instance, should certainly be sought not far from the theater.

North of the Via Egnatia, on the southern slopes of the akropolis, is a building that certainly existed in Paul's time (pl. VII,2). It is a small temple, with a pronaos and cella, built of local marble in a monumental style. It was later incorporated into the Basilica A complex and has been iden-

69. Paul Collart, "Le Théâtre de Philippes," *BCH* 52 (1928) 74–124. Recent research: Demetrios Lazaridis, "Excavations and Other Works in Eastern Macedonia," *ADelt* 16B (1960) 219 [in Greek]; idem, "Antiquities and Monuments of Eastern Macedonia," *ADelt* 17B (1961–62) 244 [in Greek]; idem, "Antiquities and Monuments of Eastern Macedonia," *ADelt* 18B (1963) 256 [in Greek]; Chaido Koukouli-Chrysantaki, "Antiquities and Monuments of Eastern Macedonia," *ADelt* 30B (1975) 284 [in Greek]; idem, "Antiquities and Monuments of Eastern Macedonia," *ADelt* 31B (1976) 299–300 [in Greek]; V. Palios, "Philippi, Ancient Theater," *ADelt* 39B (1984) 270 [in Greek]; idem, "Philippi, Ancient Theater," *ADelt* 40B (1985) 263–64 [in Greek]; idem, "Philippi, Theater," *ADelt* 41B (1986) 176–77 [in Greek]. See also C. Samiou and G. Athanassiadis, "Archaeological and Restoration Work in the Theater of Philippi," *To Archaeologiko Ergo sti Makedonia kai Thraki* 1 (1987) 353–58 [in Greek].
70. Collart and Ducrey, *Les reliefs rupestres*.
71. Collart, "Le sanctuaire des dieux égyptiens," 70–100.

tified as a heroon.[72] It dates from the fourth century BCE, and scholars have suggested that it was connected with the cult of Philipp II,[73] a hypothesis which is supported by an inscription found by Pierre Ducrey built into the wall of Basilica A not far from the heroon itself.[74] The inscription refers to the precincts of the Olympian gods and of various heroes, including two precincts of Philipp II. Sève and Weber have shown that this temple-shaped structure was included in the great building program for the forum in the Antonine period.[75]

The building popularly known as "Saint Paul's Prison" is located near the heroon (pl. VIII,1). The religious character of this area from the end of the fourth century BCE to the second century CE certainly conflicts with the notion that there could have been an actual prison here in the early Roman period. Saint Paul's Prison is in fact part of the cistern[76] of a Roman building incorporated into the complex of Basilica A. Recent research has shown that the cult of Saint Paul was transferred here after the destruction of Basil-

---

72. *BCH* 59 (1935) Chronique, 290; *BCH* 60 (1936) Chronique, 479; *BCH* 61 (1937) Chronique, 463–65; Collart, *Philippes*, 1. 177, 369–70.

73. C. Habicht, "Gottmenschtum und griechische Städte," *Zetemata* 14 (1970) 200–205; E. A. Fredricksmeyer, "Divine Honor for Philip II," *TAPA* 109 (1979) 36–61; but see also Ernest Badian, "The Deification of Alexander the Great," *Ancient Macedonian Studies in Honor of Charles F. Edson* (Thessalonike: Institute for Balkan Studies 158, 1981) 37–71, who denies the existence of a cult of Philipp either during his lifetime or after his death. This opinion is shared by F. W. Walbank in "Monarchies and Monarchic Ideas," *CAH* 7(2). 1 (1984) 87–90.

74. P. Ducrey, "Gods and Sanctuaries at Philippi in Macedonia," *Memory to D. Lazaridis*, 551–57.

75. M. Sève and P. Weber, "Le côté nord du forum de Philippes," *BCH* 110 (1986) 531–88, suggest that the building dates from the Roman period.

76. Lemerle, *Philippes*, 296–97.

ica A and particularly after the destruction of the Octagonal Church.[77]

The earliest cult center of Saint Paul, however, has been found near another pagan heroon in the center of Philippi.[78] The surviving parts of this funerary building include the burial chamber and the triple podium of a temple-shaped structure that once stood over the vaulted roof of the underground chamber (pl. IX,1). The deceased, probably a child,[79] was buried in a cist under the floor of the chamber. The name ΕΥΗΦΕΝΗΣ ΕΞΗΚΕΣΤΟΥ was incised on the lid. Rich grave offerings, consisting mainly of gold jewelry, accompanied the body. Among them were a wreath of gold oak leaves, a rhomboid gold mouth piece, a gold pendant, and a gold diadem (pl. IX,2).[80] The location of this funerary structure in the center of the city of Philippi indicates the religious character of the heroon; it was probably connected with the cult of the Great Gods on Samothrake[81] and possibly — as the gold diadem suggests — with the Egyptian gods as well.[82]

Recent excavations by Charalambos Bakirtzis have shown that this heroon (a precinct with a surrounding wall) was still a revered cult center in Roman times and certainly existed

---

77. Elli Pelekanidou, "The Traditional Prison of St Paul the Apostle at Philippi," *Kavala and the Surrounding Area,* 427–35 [in Greek].

78. Demetrios Lazaridis, "Philippi," *ADelt* 19 (1964) B3, 372–73 [in Greek].

79. The dimensions of the cist indicate that the deceased was either a child or a very short adult. See also the connection between the diadem and statuettes of children on Thasos; Rolley, "Les cultes égyptiens," 187–219.

80. *Ancient Macedonia, Exhibition Catalogue* (Athens: Ministry of Culture, 1988) nos. 373–75.

81. The name ΕΞΗΚΕΣΤΟΣ appears in a catalogue of mystes ("initiates") of Samothrake on a fragmentary votive inscription found in Philippi, Philippi Museum Inv. no. Λ25.

82. Rolley, "Les cultes égyptiens," 218.

when Paul visited Philippi.[83] The site's strong religious character survived when the religion changed; it was here that the first Christian assembly hall, dedicated to Paul, was erected, to be succeeded in the fifth century by the monumental Octagon Church.[84]

Paul and his companions went looking for those who "worshiped God" (the Jews) outside the city of Philippi (Acts 16:13). The words in the Acts of the Apostles ἐξήλθομεν ἔξω τῆς πύλης ("we went outside the gate") have been interpreted in various ways. Some scholars connect this gate with the monumental vault near the River Gangites, which was found and studied by Heuzey and Daumet (pl. VIII,2).[85] The purpose of the vault is still a subject of some controversy: was it connected with the Battle of Philippi (the hill where it was fought is not far away),[86] or did it mark the boundary of the city's *pomerium*?[87] An archaeological investigation of the monument has yet to be conducted.

Regardless, neither the identification of the πύλη with this vault nor the identification of the ποταμός with the River Gangites[88] is convincing. It seems more probable that the πύλη was the city's west gate and the ποταμός was the stream that still flows a short distance away from it.[89] Moreover, excavations in the area outside the west gate (pl. X,1) have

---

83. Pelekanidis, "Kultprobleme im Apostel-Paulus Octogon," 2. 393; idem, "Conclusions from the Excavation of the Octagon," 153–56, pl. 2; Charalambos Bakirtzis, "Paul and Philippi: The Archaeological Evidence," pp. 42–45 in this volume.
84. Pelekanidis, "Philippi," 112.
85. Heuzey and Daumet, *Mission archéologique*, 117–20, pl. II.
86. Ibid., 119–20.
87. Collart, *Philippes*, 1. 321–24.
88. Heuzey and Daumet, *Mission archéologique*, 120; Collart, *Philippes*, 1. 458–60.
89. Roger, "L'enceinte basse de Philippes," 21–41; Lemerle, *Philippes*, 25–27.

revealed a paved road, probably the Via Egnatia, bordered by grave monuments.[90] Thus, the city's *pomerium* must be sought further to the west, probably in the area of the vault. Paul and his companions would certainly have seen this impressive vault when they visited the west of the city on their way to "prayer," or when they set off along the Via Egnatia for Amphipolis.

Another structure that Paul and his companions would have seen outside the city walls is the Roman bridge that stood until recently near the village of Mavrolefki (pl. X,3).[91] On leaving Philippi for Amphipolis, they would have passed this bridge. Near it Collart has located the *mansio* "Ad Duodecimum" on the Via Egnatia,[92] mentioned in the *Itinerarium Hierosolymitanum*.[93]

Society and Cults

The population of Philippi in the Julio-Claudian period was a mixture of Greeks, Romans, native Thracians, and foreigners.[94] This Roman colony was chiefly an agricultural one, so many of the inhabitants lived in villages (*vici*, κῶμαι) or in the large farms scattered over its extensive territory.[95] They

---

90. Chaido Koukouli-Chrysantaki, "Antiquities and Monuments of Eastern Macedonia," *ADelt* 26 (1971) B2, 413; 29 (1973–74) B3, 786, pl. 577 b–g; 30 (1975) B2, 285 [in Greek].

91. Of the three bridges mentioned by Collart, *Philippes,* 2. pl. LXXXV, 1–2 (Kourovo), LXXXVI, 1 (Kadim Keupru), only the last has been saved under a modern road near the village of Symvoli. However, it has nothing to do with the Via Egnatia.

92. Collart, *Philippes,* 1. 501–2. See also the inscription mentioning *tabernae* found in the same area: P. Perdrizet, "Trois Inscriptions Latines de Roumélie," *BCH* 24 (1900) 544; Collart, *Philippes,* 1. 502 n. 1.

93. *Itinerarium Hierosolymitanum,* ed. Wesseling, 604.

94. Collart, *Philippes,* 1. 290–305; D. Kanatsoulis, "The Macedonian City," *Makedonika* 6 (1964–65) 16–28 [in Greek].

95. Papazoglou, "Le Territoire," 89–106.

included a large number of Roman veterans, to whom the emperor had given land.[96] The ruling class consisted of Romans, who were responsible for the administration of the colony. We know the names of many of Philippi's magistrates, chiefly from inscriptions dating from the second century CE.[97] The στρατηγοί mentioned in the Acts of the Apostles have been identified as the colony's *duoviri,*[98] who are also referred to as ἄρχοντες. There is no archaeological evidence relating to the ῥαβδοῦχοι,[99] but the inscriptions provide plentiful information about the administration of the colony, as also about its social structure.[100] The people — Roman, Greek, and Thracian citizens, *liberti,* slaves, and foreigners — were organized in *collegia,* usually of a religious nature.[101] Latin was already the official language in the Julio-Claudian period, but it always coexisted with Greek, until the third or fourth century CE, when the latter reappears in the inscriptions as the official language.[102]

Paul and his companions would certainly have used the bronze coins bearing the portrait of Claudius that were struck in Philippi during his reign (42–54 CE) for internal use (pl. X,2a–b).[103] There is little definite archaeological evidence

---

96. Antony and Octavian first settled *veterani* in the area of Philippi between 42 and 30 BCE: Collart, *Philippes,* 1. 234–35. Roman veterans continued to be settled in the area later on as well. See the grave stele of the legionnaire M. Tiberius Claudius Maximus, found in the modern village of Grammeni (near Drama): M. Speidel, "The Captor of Decabalus: A New Inscription of Philippi," *JRS* 60 (1970) 142–53.

97. Collart, *Philippes,* 1. 262.

98. Lemerle, *Philippes,* 32–34.

99. Ibid., 37.

100. Collart, *Philippes,* 1. 258–317.

101. Ibid., 1. 417–23; Papazoglou, "Le Territoire," 105.

102. See also *Imeriou Logoi* 6.2.3.

103. H. Gaebler, *Die antiken Münzen Nordgriechenlands* (Berlin: Preussische Akademie der Wissenschaften 3, 1935) 103, pl. XX, 16.

about private buildings dating from the time of Paul's visit. The Acts of the Apostles mentions Lydia, who, together with her household, was the first to accept the new religion. Her house must have been a large building, like the late Roman and early Christian houses recently excavated by Georgios Gounaris in the east part of the city.[104] There is also little accurately dated archaeological evidence about the cults in Philippi at this time. We know that the old gods, such as Apollo Comaeus and Artemis,[105] whom the Thasian colonists had brought with them, retained an important place in the city's religious life. Votive monuments to Apollo Comaeus have been found near the commercial agora[106] and in Basilica C,[107] while the cult of Artemis blended elements of the Greek Artemis with those of the local Thracian goddess Bendis.[108] The cult of Dionysos must also have occupied a major position in Philippi,[109] for the city was located not far away from Mount Pangaion, which was closely connected with Dionysos and his cult.[110] The cult of the hero-horseman was likewise widespread in the general area of Philippi, as is attested by votive inscriptions and

---

104. Gounaris and Velenis, "Philippi Excavation 1991 (Phase A)," 409–17.

105. François Salviat, "Une nouvelle loi thasienne," *BCH* 82 (1958) 261–63.

106. Lazaridis, *Philippi*, in "Macedonia," *ADelt* 17B (1961–62) 239 [in Greek].

107. In situ, unpublished.

108. Hesychius, s.v. Δίλογχον τὴν Βενδῖν οὕτω Κρατῖνος, ἐν Θράτταις ἐκάλεσεν. Collart, *Philippes*, 1. 430–43. See also Collart and Ducrey, *Les reliefs rupestres*, 201–27.

109. See Collart, *Philippes*, 1. 413–22.

110. Ibid., 1. 423–29, 480; Chaido Koukouli-Chrysantaki, "The Ancient Settlement of Drama and the Sanctuary of Dionysus," *Proceedings of the First Scientific Colloquium on "Drama and the Surrounding Area," Drama, November 24th–25th 1989* (Drama: Municipality of Drama, 1992) 67–86 [in Greek].

numerous votive and grave reliefs found in the city and its environs. The colony of Philippi made special votive offerings to the Sanctuary of Heros Aulonites on Pangaion,[111] and he later appeared on the city's coins as its protector.[112] At this time in Philippi, as all over the Graeco-Roman world, inhabitants worshiped not only the Greek pantheon[113] but also Roman gods,[114] local gods,[115] and foreign gods from Asia Minor[116] and Egypt,[117] as well as the cult of the Kabiroi of Samothrake, which was widespread in Macedonia by the Hellenistic period.[118] Another important cult in Colonia Augusta Iulia Philippensis was that of the emperors. Apart from the cult of Augustus and Livia, Philippi also yields evidence of the cult of Claudius,[119] which was probably already established by the time Paul arrived, although Claudius had

---

111. Votive offerings from the city of Philippi have been found in the Sanctuary of the Heros Aulonites on Pangaion; cf. C. Koukouli and D. Malamidou, "The Sanctuary of Heros Aulonites on Pangaeum," *To Archaeologiko Ergo sti Makedonia kai Thraki* 3 (1989) 553; 4 (1990) 503–11 [in Greek].

112. Oliver Picard, "Excavations by the French Archaeological School on Thasos in 1988," *To Archaeologiko Ergo sti Makedonia kai Thraki* 3 (1989) 389, pl. 10 [in Greek].

113. Collart, *Philippes*, 1. 2. 393–401.

114. Ibid., 1. 401–43.

115. Ibid., 1. 480.

116. Ibid., 1. 454–55.

117. Collart, "Le sanctuaire des dieux égyptiens," 70–100.

118. See inscription in Philippi Museum Inv. no. Λ25; D. Lazaridis, "Antiquities and Monuments of Eastern Macedonia," *ADelt* 19B (1964) B, Chronika, 372–73 [in Greek]; idem, *A Macedonian Tomb in Philippi* (in press) [in Greek]; Pelekanidis, "Kultprobleme im Apostel-Paulus Octogon," 2. 393; idem, "Conclusions from the Excavation of the Octagon," 149–58. For the cult of the Kabiroi in Thessalonike, see Giannes Touratsoglou, *Die Münzstätte von Thessaloniki in der römischen Kaiserzeit* (Deutsches Archäologisches Institut, Antike Münzen und geschnittene Steine XII; Berlin: de Gruyter, 1988) 95–96 (includes bibliography).

119. See the inscribed sarcophagus of a Claudian priest named P. C. Asper Attiarius Montanus, first seen by Heuzey and Daumet, *Mis-*

refused to accept the divine honors the Thasians tried to bestow upon him.[120]

It is evident that the cults that, through initiation and purification ceremonies, promised people a better life after death were gaining ground. The cults of Dionysos and the hero-horseman had a special place near those of the Kabiroi, the Egyptian gods, and the great goddess Cybele and her companion Attis.

There is no evidence for the worship of Mithras in Philippi, though it is archaeologically attested to in Aegean Thrace.[121] Asians living in the city certainly practiced the Asian cults.[122] One of these Asians was Lydia of Thyatira, who probably belonged to a religious group that has come to be known as the "Godfearers" and had some connection with the Jewish religion, possibly by way of the cult of Zeus Hypsistos.[123] Although no monuments of this latter cult

---

sion archéologique, in Philippi's seaport Neapolis; Kavala Museum Inv. no. Λ276.

120. C. Dunant and J. Pouilloux, *Recherches sur l'histoire et les cultes de Thasos* (Études thasiennes 5, Paris: École française d'Athènes, 1958) 66–69, no. 179; 69–70, nos. 180, 181.

121. Collart, *Philippes,* 1. 456; D. Triantaphyllos, "A Relief of Mithra Tauroctonos at Thermes in the Prefecture of Xanthi," *Thrakika Chronika* 4 (1990) 46–55 [in Greek].

122. S. Mertzidis (*Philippi* [Constantinople, 1897] 187 [in Greek]) refers to an inscription found at Philippi mentioning another "seller of purple" from Thyatira. The presence of sellers of purple in Philippi is also attested in a fragmentary inscription mentioned by Heuzey and Daumet, *Mission archéologique,* 28 (=CIL III, 664). However, Louis Robert, "Inscriptions de Philippes," *Revue de Philologie* 13 (1939) 136–50, challenges the authenticity of Mertzidis's inscription. Lemerle (*Philippes,* 28–29) does not entirely agree with Robert.

123. Acts 16:14. Cf. M. Tacheva, "Dem Hypsistos geweihte Denkmäler in Thrakien," *Thracia* 4 (1977) 271–301. The publication of the Jewish inscriptions from Aphrodisias leaves no doubt about the existence of this group in the Jewish communities; see Reynolds and Tannenbaum, *Jews and Godfearers at Aphrodisias.*

have yet been located in the city of Philippi itself,[124] it was widely practiced in the surrounding area.[125] The cult of Zeus Hypsistos is not always connected with Jews, but the presence of Jews in Philippi is indicated by the reference in the Acts to a place where προσευχή ("prayer") occurred.[126] According to the Book of Acts, Paul and his companions were looking for a Jewish meeting place as soon as they reached Philippi. As Acts 17:1 tells, they did the same later in Thessalonike and then in Beroia.[127] In Philippi, Paul sought the Jews outside the city, where he had been told there was a προσευχή.[128]

---

124. For the cult of Zeus, see Collart, *Philippes,* 1. 393–94; Collart and Ducrey, *Les reliefs rupestres,* 159–63, 237–40.

125. See two votive inscriptions to Zeus Hypsistos from a sanctuary dedicated to him in an ancient marble quarry situated to the east of ancient Neapolis (Kavala), near the modern village of Chalkeron (Kavala Museum Inv. no. 2); G. Bakalakis, "Thracian Engravings to Zeus Hypsistos," *Thrakika* 6 (1935) 302–8 [in Greek] (Kavala Museum Inv. no. Λ1382); M. Nikolaïdou-Patera, "A Local Sanctuary of Zeus Hypsistos near Kavala," *Thrakiki Epetirida* 7 (1987–90) 213–21 [in Greek]. See also the votive relief of an eagle with an inscription from the village of Nikesiani near Philippi (Kavala Museum Inv. no. Λ896, unpublished).

126. Acts 16:13; cf. Lemerle, *Philippes,* 23.

127. Acts 17:10–14. The earliest inscription found so far that mentions a synagogue in the city has been dated by Feissel (*Recueil des inscriptions,* no. 295) to the fourth or fifth century CE.

128. Concerning προσευχή, see Josephus *AJ* 14.10.23. According to recent research, the προσευχή was the oldest designation of a Jewish assembly hall. In Saint Paul's time, the synagogues of the Diaspora were still inside private or public buildings; see J. Gutman, *The Synagogue: Studies in Origin, Archaeology and Architecture* (New York: Ktav, 1975); Kee, "The Transformation of the Synagogue," 1–24 (including bibliography); L. Michael White, "The House and the Synagogue in the Aegean" (lecture at the Byzantine Colloquium at the Ephoreia of Byzantine Antiquities of Eastern Macedonia and Thrace, Kavala, 1988).

Epimeter: The Synagogue of Philippi

Hitherto, the presence of Jews in Philippi was attested only
by this reference in the Acts of the Apostles, but a recent
find in Philippi's west cemetery has, for the first time, confirmed the existence of a synagogue in the city (pl. XI). It
is a grave stele of local marble, narrowing towards the bottom and with a curved top. The surface of the sides and
back is roughly finished. The inscription on the front is well
preserved.

Philippi Museum Inv. no. Λ1529. Dimensions: height
0.90 m; width above 0.70 m; width below 0.58 m; thickness
0.10–0.15 m; height of letters 0.03–0.055 m.

Ivy leaf	
ΝΙΚΟΣΤΡΑΤΟ(Σ)	Νικόστρατο(ς)
ΑΥΡ.ΟΞΥΧΟΛΙΟΣ	Αὐρ(ήλιος) Ὀξυχόλιος
ΕΑΥΤΟ ΚΑΤΑΣΚΕΥ	ἑαυτῶ κατασκεύ
ΒΑΣΑ ΤΟ ΧΑΜΩΣΟ	βασα τὸ χαμώσο
ΡΟΝ ΤΟΥΤΩ. ΟΣ ΑΝ ΔΕ	ρον τούτω. ὃς ἂν δὲ
ΕΤΕΡΩΝ ΝΕΚΥΝ ΚΑΤΑΘΕ	ἑτέρων νέκυν καταθέ
ΣΕ ΔΩΣΙ ΠΡΟΣΤΕΙΜΟΥ ΤΗ ΣΥ	σε(ι) δώσι προστείμου τῆ συ
ΝΑΓΩΓΗ *ΜΡ	ναγωγῆ *ΜΡ

Translation:

Nikostratos Aurelios Oxycholios himself furnished this
flat tomb/grave (and) if someone lays down (on it)
a dead body of others, he will give (a fine) to the
synagogue.

This tombstone was evidently erected on the grave of a Jew
named Nikostratos Aurelios Oxycholios. The text decrees
that the penalty for violating the grave be a fine payable to
the local synagogue.

This Jew has a Greek *cognomen* (surname), a Roman

nomen gentis (gentilicium "family name"), and second Greek *cognomen* as *supernomen* or *agnomen.* It was very common for Jews in the Roman Empire to use the Greek language and to have Greek names.[129] Evidence available from other Macedonian cities where Jews lived, such as Beroia,[130] Thessalonike,[131] and Stoboi,[132] as also from other areas, such as the Aegean islands,[133] Asia Minor,[134] Egypt,[135] Cyrene,[136]

---

129. See *CII,* passim; Louis Robert, "Un corpus des inscriptions juives," *Hellenica* 3 (1946) 90–108. The Jews of the Diaspora used Greek as their official language, and they preferred Greek names; see Victor Tcherikover, *Hellenistic Civilization and the Jews* (Philadelphia: Jewish Publication Society, 1959) 346–47; see also E. Schuerer, *The History of the Jewish People in the Age of Jesus Christ (175 B.C.E.–35 C.E.)* (New English version revised and edited by G. Vermes et al.; Edinburgh: T. & T. Clark, 1986) 3. 164–72.

130. Tataki, *Ancient Beroea,* 454–55. Two grave inscriptions have been found in Veria (Beroia). They date from the fourth or fifth century CE, and the earlier one contains a reference to a "synagogue"; see Feissel, *Recueil des inscriptions,* 243–45, nos. 294, 295.

131. Feissel, *Recueil des inscriptions,* 24–25; P. M. Nigdelis, "The Sarcophagus of M. Aurelius Jacob: New Inscriptional Evidence for the Jewish Community of Thessaloniki" (paper presented at the Third International Conference on Macedonia ["Inscriptions from Macedonia"], Aristotle University of Thessalonike, 8–12 December 1993; in press [in Greek]); idem, "Synagogen," 297–306.

132. James Wiseman and D. Mano-Zissi, "Excavations at Stoboi 1970," *AJA* 5 (1971) 406–11; 6 (1972) 407–24; James Wiseman, *Stoboi: A Guide to the Excavations* (Belgrade, 1973) 17, 30–36.

133. A. Thomas Kraabel, "The Diaspora Synagogue: Archaeological and Epigraphical Evidence," *ANRW* 2.19.1 (1979) 477–510; L. Michael White, "The Delos Synagogue Revisited: Recent Field Work in the Graeco-Roman Diaspora," *HTR* 80 (1987) 133–60; idem, "The House and the Synagogue in the Aegean."

134. Trebilco, *Jewish Communities in Asia Minor.*

135. P. M. Fraser, *Ptolemaic Alexandria* (2 vols.; New York and Oxford: Oxford University Press, 1972) 1. 57.

136. S. Appelbaum, *Greeks and Jews in Ancient Cyrene* (Leiden: Brill, 1979) 150–52, 163.

and Italy,[137] strongly suggests that the Jews became sufficiently Hellenized to adopt Greek names and sufficiently Romanized to receive Roman *gentilicia*. This does not mean, however, that they were fully integrated with the local population.[138] The absence of a Roman *praenomen* (first name) before the *gentilicium* Aurelius, with a Greek *cognomen* (Nikostratos) in its stead, is unusual.[139] The *gentilicium* proves that this Philippian Jew was a Roman citizen, who probably took Roman citizenship through Caracalla's edict of 212 CE.[140] Despite its meaning, the *nomen* Oxycholios is not a typical *agnomen (supernomen)* because the words ὁ καί are missing.[141] The name Oxycholios comes from the Greek adjective ὀξύχολος,[142] which means "quick-tempered." The *nomen* Oxycholios is encountered both in the East and the West,[143] for Christians and pagans alike, from at least the third century CE onwards. The only Jewish examples have been found in the Aphrodisias inscription, where it occurs in the list five times.[144] According to the editors, Oxycholios belongs in the category of names denoting qualities commonly admired in the ancient world, such as "nobility" (Εὐγένιος) or "high

137. H. J. Leon, *The Jews of Ancient Rome* (Philadelphia: Jewish Publication Society, 1960) 117–18.
138. Trebilco, *Jewish Communities in Asia Minor,* 173–85.
139. Salomies, *Die römischen Vornamen,* 406.
140. *Constitutio Antoniana* of 212 CE.
141. Kajanto, *Supernomina,* 5–11; see also J. Juster, *Les Juifs dan l'empire romain: Leur condition juridique, économique et sociale* (Paris: Paul Geuther, 1914) 22.
142. Ὀξύχολος, Solon 12.26; Sophocles *Ant.,* 955; *Anth. Pal.* 9. 127. Τὸ ὀξύχολον = ὀξυχολία, Lucian *Fugitivi* 1. Ὀξυχολία, Ephraem Syrus, vol. 3.221.
143. H. Solin, *Die griechischen Personennamen in Rom: Ein Namenbuch* (New York: de Gruyter, 1982) 778.
144. Reynolds and Tannenbaum, *Jews and Godfearers at Aphrodisias,* 103, no. 51; also 93–115; see also *SEG* 35 (1986) no. 1987.

spirits" (Γοργόνιος, Όξυχόλιος).[145] A pejorative meaning for Oxycholios, however, seems more probable.[146] The text is typical of grave inscriptions both in Philippi and elsewhere in Macedonia and Greece:

ἑαυτῶ κατασκεύ
βασα τὸ χαμώσο
ρον τοῦτω

The word χαμόσωρον also appears as χαμοσόριον,[147] σορός, χαμόσορον, and χαμοσόριον. These words are all used to mean "grave" in grave inscriptions of the late Roman period.[148]

Ὅς ἂν δὲ
ἑτέρων νέκυν καταθέσε(ι)[149]

145. Reynolds and Tannenbaum, *Jews and Godfearers at Aphrodisias*, 96.
146. Kajanto, *Supernomina*, 20.
147. In the two inscriptions from Philippi (Feissel, *Recueil des inscriptions*, nos. 231, 232), it is better to read χαμόσορ[ον]rather than χαμοσόρ[ιον]. The term χαμόσορον or χαμοσόριον is a late one. It appears in pagan funeral inscriptions — for instance, in a tomb inscription in Cilicia (Rudolph Heberdey-Wilhelm, *Reisen in Kilikien* [Wien: In commission bei C. Gerold's Sohn, 1896] no. 90) and in a tomb inscription from Maronia (S. Reinach, "Antiquités de Maronée et d'Abdère," *BCH* 5 [1881] 91, no. 7) — but more commonly in early Christian tomb inscriptions. See Feissel, *Recueil des inscriptions*, 195; I. Meimaris and Ch. Bakirtzis, *Greek Late Roman and Early Christian Inscriptions from W. Thrace* (Komotine: Supplement of Thrakike Epeteris no. 1, 1994) nos. 1 and 28. *Chamosorion*, in Constantine Porphyrogenitus, *The Ceremonies*, CB 646, 17.
148. In Jewish inscriptions it also appears in the form ἐνσόριον (place for a sarcophagus); see the inscription from Smyrna, κατασκεύασεν τὸ ἐνσόριον, in Trebilco, *Jewish Communities in Asia Minor*, 104.
149. The verb κατατίθημι is a very common one: see inscriptions from Philippi in Feissel, *Recueil des inscriptions*, no. 231: εἰ δέ τις τολμήσει ἕτερον σκήνωμα καταθέσθαι. See also ibid., no. 232; also inscriptions from Thessalonike, e.g., Edson, *IG* 10, no. 524: ὅστις ἂν ἕτερος μετὰ τὸ ἡμᾶς

This is another standard expression; it uses ἄν instead of εἰ for the conditional, poetic words like νέκυν, and the common verb κατατίθημι.

Δώσι προστείμου τῆ συ
ναγωγῆ

This expression is often encountered in grave inscriptions, where one usually finds τῆ πόλει or τῷ ταμείῳ.[150] In Jewish inscriptions, the adjective ἁγιωτάτη applied to the synagogue[151] corresponds to the adjective ἱερώτατον applied to the ταμεῖον.[152]

καταθέσται, δώσει τῆ πόλει; no. 525: ὃς ἂν δὲ ἕτερος καταθῆτε μετὰ τὸ ἡμᾶς κατατεθῆσαι, δώσει τῆ πόλει; or an inscription from Thasos, Dunant and Pouilloux, Études thasiennes 5 (1958) no. 246: μηδένα δὲ ἕτερον κατάθεσται (third century CE); or Christian inscriptions from Palestine and Asia Minor, SEG 1978, nos. 1395–97 (sixth century CE).

150. For the phrase δώσει προστείμου, see the inscription from West Macedonia in Touratsoglou and Rizakis, Inscriptions, no. 116: εἰ δέ τις πιράσι δώσι προστίμου τῷ εἰερωτάτῳ ταμίῳ (265/6 CE); or from Thessalonike in Edson, IG 10, no. 531: ἐὰν δέ τις ἕτερος μετὰ τὴν ἐμὴν τελευτὴν ἕτερον καταθῆτε δώσει προστείμου τῷ ταμείῳ. See also an inscription from Nicomedia in Robert, "Inscriptions juives," 391.

151. Inscription from Philadelphia, Lydia, in Trebilco, Jewish Communities in Asia Minor, 162: Τῆ ἁγιωτάτη συναγωγῆ τῶν Ἑβραίων. See also an inscription from Beroia in Feissel, Recueil des inscriptions, no. 295: (ἐάν) τις ἀνύξη τὸν τάφον δώση τῆ ἁγιωτάτη συναγω(γῆ); and one from Thessaly in Louis Robert, "Incriptions grecques de Sidè en Pamphylie," Revue de Philologie 32 (1958), 43 n. 4: ἐὰ(ν) δέ τεις τούτου τὸν τάφον ἀνορύξη δώσι τῆ ἁγιοτάτη συναγωγῆ δηναρίων μυριάδας δέκα. For the adjective ἁγιωτάτη (συναγωγή), see Robert, "Un corpus des inscriptions juives," 105–6.

152. The word tameion refers to the imperial fiscus. The phrase τῷ ἱερωτάτῳ ταμείῳ appears in pagan inscriptions: Touratsoglou and Rizakis, Inscriptions, no. 116. Louis Robert, "Aphrodisias," Hellenica 13 (1965) 211–12, with reference to the (ἁγιωτάτη) συναγωγῆ or τῷ ἔθνει τῶν Ἰουδαίων. Trebilco, Jewish Communities in Asia Minor, 104 (inscription from Smyrna): εἰ δέ τις τολμήσει δώσει τῷ ἱερωτάτῳ ταμείῳ δηνάρια φ καὶ τὸ ἔθνει τῶν Ἰουδαίων. The adjectives ἱερώτατον (ταμεῖον) or ἁγιωτάτη (συναγωγή) may be missing; cf. inscription from Nicomedia in Robert,

Regarding the fine referred to in the inscription, there are three possible interpretations of the amount of the *poena:* *MP, *M(ύ)P(ια), and *M(υριάδας)P. Although fourth-century grave inscriptions have been found in the area of Philippi with low *poenae* (such as *CCXXXX)[153] and although the reading *M(ύ)P(ια) cannot be ruled out,[154] the most probable reading seems to me to be *M(υριάδας) P.[155] Such a high sum might be expected in the late third century or fourth century CE, which was a period of mounting inflation in the Roman Empire.[156] A *poena* of one million *denarii,* although high, is not unique. A *poena* of this amount is mentioned in a grave inscription from Thessalonike,[157] and an inscription from Gallipoli refers to μυριάδες τριακόσιαι.[158]

Certain features of the inscription itself point to the end of the third century or fourth century CE — the disappearance

---

"Inscriptions juives," 387: καὶ δώσει τῇ συναγωγῇ (δηνάρια) α΄ καί τῷ ταμείῳ (δηνάρια) φ. Apart from ἔθνος and συναγωγή, the words κατοικία and λαὸς (Ἰουδαίων) are also used: Nigdelis, "Synagogen," 304 nn. 44, 45. L. H. Kant, "Jewish Inscriptions in Greek and Latin," *ANRW* 2.20.2 (1987) 705.

153. *ADelt* 23 (1968) B2, 356, pl. 303a.

154. Touratsoglou and Rizakis, *Inscriptions,* 1. 117; see *MP = *M(ύ)P(ια).

155. For the sums paid as *poenae,* see G. Millet, "Recherches au Mont Athos," *BCH* 29 (1905) 62 n. 5; T. Pekary, "Studien zur römischen Währungs- und Finanzgeschichte," *Historia* 8 (1959) 460–63; A. P. Christophilopoulou, *Nomika Epigraphica* (Athens: Christophilopoulos, 1977) 9–49 [in Greek].

156. Nigdelis, "Synagogen," 299 nn. 13, 14, with relevant bibliography.

157. Edson, *IG* 10. 2,1 no. 591: μυριάδας ἑκατὸν λ΄ ἁπλᾶς. The word ἁπλᾶς may account for the extremely heavy *poena* in this inscription; the *poena* here (as also in other grave inscriptions) has to be paid in ἁπλᾶς, which, in direct contrast to λαμπράς, can mean "worn-out coins." For the word λαμπράς, see Nigdelis, "Synagogen," 301–2.

158. See *IGRR* 1. 819, where reference is made to *poenae* of 3,000,000 and 1,000,000 *denarii* to be paid to the ἱερὸν ταμεῖον and the πόλις, respectively.

of the Roman *praenomen,* for instance,[159] the iotacizing of δώσι, the presence of the β after ευ,[160] the use of the word χαμώσορον[161] — as do external indications, such as the form of the letters and of the tombstone itself.[162] However, the extremely high *poena* — if the reading *Μ(υριάδας)Ρ is correct — precludes a date at the very beginning of the fourth century CE.[163]

This tombstone dates from much later than Saint Paul's time, but it serves as an important archaeological commentary on the Acts of the Apostles, offering the first epigraphical evidence of the existence of an organized Jewish community in the city of Philippi in the late third century CE.[164] Like the Jewish community in Thessalonike,[165] it also included Roman citizens among its members. Unlike the Thessalonian Μ(άρκος) Α(ὐρήλιος) Ἰακώβ ὁ καὶ Εὐτύχιος (Marcus Aurelius Jacob the very fortunate), the Philippian

159. Salomies, *Die römischen Vornamen,* 406; Nigdelis, "Synagogen," 299.

160. For iotacism, see Nigdelis, "Synagogen," 299 n. 9. For the use of β instead of ευ, see Louis Robert, "Inscriptions juives," n. 11; *SEG* 37 (1991) no. 1287: mosaic inscription from Cilicia (Anemurion), dated ca. 450–500 CE, containing the word ἐβλαβής. The presence of both ευ and β is a mistake.

161. For the use of the word χαμόσορον in early Christian inscriptions, see Feissel, *Recueil des inscriptions,* nos. 231 and 232.

162. See also the letters of the two inscriptions from Philippi dated to the fourth century CE in ibid., no. 231.

163. At the very beginning of the fourth century CE, the situation changed with the reforms introduced by Diocletian. Soon, however, inflation returned.

164. The presence of Jews in Macedonia is attested by Philo *Leg.* 36 (281). The existing archaeological evidence from Thessalonike, Beroia, and Stoboi dates from no earlier than the second century CE; see D. Kanatsoulis, "The Macedonian City: Part I," *Makedonika* 4 (1955) 261–64; Tataki, *Ancient Beroea; Nigdelis,* "Synagogen," 303 n. 37; see also E. M. Smallwood, *The Jews under Roman Rule from Pompey to Diocletian* (Leiden: Brill, 1981) 122.

165. Nigdelis, "Synagogen," 299.

Νικόστρατο(ς) Αὐρ(ήλιος) Ὀξυχόλιος (Nikostratos Aurelius the ?bad-tempered?) did not bear the Roman *praenomen* Marcus.[166]

The name Σίμων Σμυρναῖος, in another grave inscription recently found in Philippi, probably belonged to another member of the city's Jewish community.[167] It too may be dated to the late third or early fourth century, and this Simon was evidently a native of the city of Smyrna, which had a flourishing Jewish community.[168]

The date of this first appearance of any reference to a synagogue in grave inscriptions in Philippi, as well as Macedonia, agrees with the available literary and archaeological evidence from Palestine and the Diaspora, where there is no reference to the synagogue as a religious meeting place before the third century CE.[169]

---

166. About the M. Aurelii in Thessalonike, see D. Samsaris, "The Individual Grants of the Roman Citizenship (Civitas Romana) and Its Expansion in the Roman Province of Macedonia (I. The Case of Thessaloniki, Capital of the Province)," *Makedonika* 26 (1987–88) 319; see also Nigdelis, "Synagogen," 299 nn. 10–12.

167. Philippi Museum Inv. no. Λ1776. Dimensions: height 0.55 m; width 0.44 m; thickness 0.11 m; height of letters 0.04–0.05 m; space between lines 0.04 m. The name ΣΙΜΩΝ is also used by Greeks, but more often by Jews; see P. M. Fraser and E. Matthews, *A Lexicon of Greek Personal Names* (Oxford: Clarendon, 1987) s.v. Σίμων; *CII*, nos. 165, 166, 176, 403.

168. Trebilco, *Jewish Communities in Asia Minor,* 35. For the name Σίμων, see also Rudolf Horn, "Hellenistische Bildwerke auf Samos," *Samos XII* (Bonn: Deutsches Archäologisches Institut, Habelt, 1972) 141.

169. Martin Hengel, "Proseuche und Synagoge, Jüdische Gemeinde, Gotteshaus und Gottesdienst in der Diaspora und Palästina," in *Tradition und Glaube: Das frühe Christentum in seiner Umwelt, Festgabe für K. G. Kuhn zum 65. Geburtstag,* ed. G. Jeremias et al. (Göttingen: Vandenhoeck & Ruprecht, 1971) 15. Kee, "The Transformation of the Synagogue," 5–14.

2

PAUL AND PHILIPPI

The Archaeological Evidence

Charalambos Bakirtzis

The Acts of the Apostles (16:11–40) describes the city of Philippi, its buildings, and its social organization. Outside the city walls, by the river, there was a synagogue; within the city was an agora where the rulers met; the city jail also had an "inner prison"; and the citizens lived with their households in spacious dwellings. Philippi as it is now bears very little relationship to the city that Paul visited in 49/50 CE. The ruins we see today (pl. IV)[1] — the agora, the basilicas, the Octagon — belong to structures that were built long after he visited Philippi. There remains intact from Paul's time, however, the general site and the surrounding ridges formed by Mounts Pangaion, Symbolon, and Orbelos, as well as the

---

1. Collart, *Philippes;* Lemerle, *Philippes;* Stylianos Pelekanidis, "The Extramural Early Christian Basilica of Philippi," *AEphem* 1955, 114–79, reprinted in idem, *Studien,* 333–94; idem, "Conclusions from the Excavation of the Octagon," 149–58; idem, "Philippi," 101–25; R. F. Hoddinott, *Early Byzantine Churches in Macedonia and Southern Serbia* (London: Macmillan, 1963) 99–106 (Extra Muros Basilica), 169–73 (Basilica A), 188–93 (Basilica B); Demetrios Pallas, *Les monuments paléochrétiens découverts de 1959 à 1973* (Sussidi allo Studio delle Antiquità Cristiane 5; Vatican City: Pontificio Istituto di Archeologia Cristiana, 1977) 106–20; G. Lavas, "The Cities of the 'Christian Basilicas': A Contribution to the Town Planning of Eastern Illyricum," in *Actes du Xe Congrès International d'Archéologie Chrétienne,* 591–95.

general landscape, though the now fertile plain was largely marshland in the early Christian period. My paper, then, examines archaeological finds connected with Paul that date from long after his visit.

In the center of Philippi was the agora, an open square constructed in the second century CE and surrounded by porticoes, public buildings, and temples (fig. 4).[2] When Paul Collart and, later, Demetrios Lazaridis excavated this large complex, they found no evidence that Christian structures had been built on top of Roman ones, but they discovered that the nearby Basilica B, for instance, was erected on the site of the city's Roman gymnasium.[3] The surviving early Christian columns and Justinian Ionic impost capitals (pl. XII,1) indicate that the porticoes were repaired in the Christian period,[4] and the grooves in the paved floor in front of the northwest pagan temple (pl. XII,2) suggest that its dilapidated facade was propped up with timber beams, though it was not possible to restore it properly. I suspect that in early Christian times Philippi was divided into separate communities and neighborhoods along religious lines, and I am inclined to believe that, in a spirit of peaceful coexistence, the pagans retained the agora as their social center, while the Christians created their own centers in the area surrounding the agora,[5] such as the region east of the agora.

It was here that Stylianos Pelekanidis excavated the Oc-

2. Collart, *Philippes*, 1. 329–62; Lazaridis, *Philippi: Roman Colony*, 34–36; Lazaridis, *Philippi*, 25–29.

3. Lemerle, *Philippes*, 421–24; Lazaridis, *Philippi: Roman Colony*, 34–36; Lazaridis, *Philippi*, 25–29.

4. Vassiliki Vemi, *Les chapiteaux ioniques à imposte de Grèce à l'époque paléochrétienne* (BCH Sup. 17; Athens: École française d'Athènes, 1989) 159, pl. 57.

5. This was also the case in Athens (Alison Franz, "From Paganism to Christianity in the Temples of Athens," *DOP* 19 [1965] 193–94) and Paphos on Cyprus.

tagon, Philippi's cathedral church, and the complex of buildings connected with it (pl. XIII).[6] It was an internally octagonal church (fig. 5,1) with a narthex (fig. 5,2), which was approached through a three-aisled atrium-like portico (fig. 5,3) with an entrance on the Via Egnatia, the city's *decumanus maximus* (main road). To the north of the Octagon stood the fountain, which is a shallow open basin (fig. 7,1), a central chamber (fig. 7,3) for certain Christian cult rituals, and a complete four-part baptistery.

This baptistery is composed of an *apodyterion* (dressing room; fig. 7,2a), a catechumens' room (fig. 7,2b), a *photisterion* (place of illumination), where the baptismal font was located (fig. 7,2c), and a *chrismarion,* where participants were anointed with oil immediately after baptism took place (fig. 7,2d). Individuals about to be baptized would enter from the *phiale* (fountain) into the apodyterion through an anteroom. In the apodyterion, a small, narrow room with a wardrobe in the center, they disrobed and put on white chitons. Passing into the *katechumenon,* which was a larger room with seats for the catechists (baptismal instructors), they underwent instruction. Following this, they were baptized in the photisterion and then anointed in the chrismarion. The presence of a complete four-part baptistery in the Octagon complex and the absence of a baptistery in any of the other Philippian churches indicate that the Octagon

---

6. Preliminary reports were published by Stylianos Pelekanidis in *Praktika Archaeologikis Etaireias* (Athens) 1958, 84–89; 1959, 49–58; 1960, 76–94; 1961, 69–80; 1962, 169–78; 1963, 81–88; 1964, 172–78; 1966, 47–58; 1967, 70–82; 1968, 72–79; 1969, 42–53; 1970, 55–65; 1971, 72–85; 1972, 73–85; 1973, 55–69; 1974, 65–72; 1975, 91–102; 1976, 115–29; 1977, 66–77; 1978, 64–72; 1979, 90–99; see also ibid., 1981, 8–17; 1982, 31–42; 1983/A, 30–34; idem, "Excavations in Philippi," *Balkan Studies* 8 (1967) 123–26, reprinted in idem, *Studien,* 335–99; see also the literature quoted above in n. 1; furthermore, Pelekanidou and Mentzos, "The Octagon," 597–606.

complex was the bishop's church in Philippi. Between the baptistery and the Via Egnatia was a *balneum* (bath; fig. 5,4), which functioned from the time of Augustus onwards.[7] A large building to the east of the Octagon complex was the bishop's palace[8] (fig. 5,5).

To the west of the Octagon — that is, west of the narthex and the three-aisled portico — a number of rooms (fig. 5,6) and a large courtyard (fig. 5,7) have been excavated. It has been suggested that the former were storerooms and workshops and that the latter was an atrium of the Octagon. However, the fact that the courtyard and the narthex of the Octagon lie on very different levels and that there was no direct access between them casts doubt on this theory. The paved, open-air courtyard had a magnificent entrance (fig. 5,8) on the Commercial Road, which was the main south *decumanus;* it also had two porticoes (fig. 5,7a), and an impressive phiale (fig. 5,7b) constructed from marble taken from a second-century building in the agora. Three doorways led from the north portico to the complex of rooms, which did not communicate with the Octagon. I do not believe that the courtyard was an atrium, or that the rooms were storerooms and workshops. Rather, they belonged to a guesthouse for pilgrims, approached from the Commercial Road, with a number of rooms and a courtyard. The courtyard gave indirect and controlled access to the narthex of the Octagon by means of two corner staircases and doors. Frequent use of the Octagon by worshipers is suggested by one worshiper's engraving on the western marble stylobate of the three-aisled portico:

---

7. Gounaris, *Balneum*, passim.

8. Charalambos Bakirtzis, "The Bishop's Palace in Philippi," in *Kavala and the Surrounding Area 2,* 149–57; V. Müller-Wiener, "Riflessioni sulle caratteristiche dei palazzi episcopali," *Felix Ravenna* 125–26 (1983) 124–27.

Κ(ύρι)ε βοήθη τοῦ δούλου σου Πέτρου, ἀμήν

Lord, help your servant Peter. Amen.

Why, however, was an octagonal church — a very unusual form for an early Christian church — built on this site in Philippi, and what shrine did the guesthouse serve? A systematic excavation revealed a long, three-part building, consisting of a narthex, *naos* (nave), and sanctuary, which were lying under the floor of the north part of the Octagon (pl. XIV).[9] Its mosaic floor depicts a fruit-bearing tree with birds (symbolic representations of Paradise), geometric patterns, and inscriptions.[10] On the eastern side of the nave, in front of the sanctuary, an inscription was found (pl. XV). In gold, red, and grey tesserae it reads:

Πο[ρφύ]ριος ἐπίσκο
πος τὴ[ν κ]έντησιν τῆς βασιλικῆ
ς Παύλο[υ ἐπ]οίησεν ἐν Χρ(ιστ)ῷ

Bishop Porphyrios made the embroidery of Paul's basilica in Christ.[11]

There was only one known Philippian bishop with this name; Porphyrios was the bishop of Philippi who signed the proceedings of the Council of Serdica in 342/43 or

---

9. Pelekanidis, "Excavation of Philippi," *Praktika Archaeologikis Etaireias* (Athens) 1975, 98; 1978, 70; idem, "Philippi," 108; Pelekanidou and Mentzos, "The Octagon," 597–600.

10. P. Assimakopoulou-Atzaka, "The Early Christian Mosaic Floors of Eastern Illyricum," *Actes du Xe Congrès International d'Archéologie Chrétienne*, 406–7, 513–17; Pelekanidis, "Excavation of Philippi," *Praktika Archaeologikis Etaireias* (Athens) 1975, 98–101; 1976, 128–29.

11. Pelekanidis, "Excavation of Philippi," *Praktika Archaeologikis Etaireias* (Athens) 1975, 101–2; idem, "Philippi," 108; Feissel, *Recueil des inscriptions*, no. 226.

343/44 CE.[12] "Embroidery" refers to the mosaic floor,[13] and "basilica" is here the designation of an assembly hall.[14] We may conclude, then, that after the so-called Edict of Milan in 313 CE, Philippi's first public Christian assembly hall was erected on the central site just to the east of the agora, and it was dedicated to the memory of Saint Paul.[15] The dates for Porphyrios's service as bishop make this building in the Balkans the earliest known public assembly hall for Christians that can be dated with some certainty.

The church's north side adjoined the south side of a Hellenistic building that consisted of a temple above ground and a subterranean Macedonian tomb underneath it. This was the *heroon* (memorial shrine) of a local hero.[16] The type and location of this tomb in Philippi's center, just east of the agora, shows that the grave was not that of a common individual but of a famous person or city hero. That the tomb is indeed a heroon is indicated by the preserved remains of a three-stepped crepis foundation of the temple-shaped superstructure above the burial chamber, as well as by the courtyard and enclosure around the area — the specific marking for a sacred temenos.

The south wall of the Christian assembly hall also dates from an earlier period and was in fact part of the original

---

12. Valerie Abrahamsen, "Bishop Porphyrios and the City of Philippi in the Early Fourth Century," *VC* 43 (1989) 80–85.

13. G. W. Lampe, *A Patristic Greek Lexicon*, s.v. κέντησις.

14. For the meaning of the term *basilica* as a Christian assembly hall in the beginning of the fourth century, see A. K. Orlandos, *The Timber-Roofed Early Christian Basilica in the Mediterranean Basin* (Library of the Archaeological Society of Athens 35; Athens, 1952) 19 [in Greek]; Charles Delvoye, "Basilica," in *Reallexikon zur byzantinischen Kunst*, 1. 514–24.

15. There can be no doubt that the "Paul" mentioned in the inscription is indeed the apostle; Pelekanidis, "Kultprobleme im Apostel-Paulus Octogon," 2. 393–97. Gounaris (*Balneum*, 57) suggested that "Paul" refers to an unknown martyr.

16. Chaido Koukouli-Chrysantaki, pp. 20–21 in this volume.

enclosure for the heroon. Thus this Christian assembly hall was evidently built into the southern section of the courtyard or sacred temenos of the pagan heroon (fig. 6). Another inscription was found on the mosaic floor of the narthex:

Χριστέ, βωήθι τὸ δούλου σου Πρίσκου σὺν παντὶ τοῦ οἴκου αὐτοῦ

Christ, help your servant Priscus with all his household.

The inscription's N-S orientation indicates that it was intended to be read by those entering the Christian assembly hall through a northern entrance from the courtyard of the heroon. This implies that at some point in the early fourth century CE, at least at the time of Bishop Porphyrios, the pagan and Christian sanctuaries were functioning simultaneously side by side.

This twofold function, Christian and pagan, was not an unusual phenomenon in the middle of the fourth century, after the so-called Edict of Milan (313 CE):[17] a martyrium containing relics of Saint Babylas was built in 351 near the Temple of Apollo and the spring of Kastalia at Daphne, a suburb of Antioch. Christian martyria were also functioning or under construction in 362 near the Temple of Apollo at Didyma. At Salamis on Cyprus the tombs of Christian martyrs were situated close to a temple of Jupiter.[18] In 351 Julian

17. Timothy Gregory, "The Survival of Paganism in Christian Greece: A Critical Essay," *AJP* 107 (1986) 229–42 and, especially for Philippi, 237.

18. G. Downey, "The Shrine of St. Babylas at Antioch and Daphne," in *Antioch-on-the-Orontes, II, The Excavations 1933–1936*, ed. R. Stillwell (Princeton: Princeton University Press, 1938) 45. Sozomenus *Hist. eccl.* 5.20; *Patrologia Graeca* 67. 1280: ἐπὶ τιμῇ μαρτύρων εὐκτηρίους οἴκους εἶναι πλησίον τοῦ ναοῦ Διδυμαίου Ἀπόλλωνος, ὃς πρὸ τῆς Μιλήτου ἐστίν, ἔγραψε (ὁ Ἰουλιανός)...τῷ ἡγεμόνι Καρίας, εἰ μὲν ὄροφόν τε καὶ τράπεζαν ἱερὰν ἕξουσι, πυρὶ καταφλέξαι εἰ δὲ ἡμίεργά ἐστι τὰ οἰκοδομήματα, ἐκ βάθρων ἀνασκάψαι. Polybii episcopi Rhinocorurorum *Vitae S. Epiphanii*

the Apostate learned, to his surprise, that the Christians of Troy held their Christian martyrs and pagan heroes in equal veneration.[19]

It is not at all strange that one cult was linked with another, given the climate of religious freedom and spiritual restlessness that had prevailed in Philippi since the time of Paul and Polycarp.[20] Recent excavations have uncovered, just under the floor of the Christian assembly hall, the walls of chambers that were attached to the heroon and probably served some devotional purpose. This suggests that the Christians, having asked and received official permission to build their assembly hall adjacent to and in the courtyard of the local heroon, were simply repeating a practice already followed by other religious communities in Philippi. The only difference was that the Christian precinct of buildings was both larger and more enduring than that of the pagans.

Pelekanidis demonstrated that in the case of the Octagon of Philippi, pagan hero worship was supplanted by the cult of the Christian martyrs.[21] He also showed that the preservation of the underground section of the pagan heroon among the Octagon's auxiliary rooms as the center of the Christian cult bears out A. von Harnack's and E. Lucius's theories that the church became increasingly Hellenized from Paul's time onwards, juxtaposing the cult of the Christian martyrs with

episcopi Constantiensis episcopi Patrologia Graeca 41.89: ἦν δὲ ναὸς ἐκεῖνος ἀρχαῖος, ὅστις ἐκαλεῖτο Διὸς Ἀσφάλεια.

19. Julian, Oeuvres complètes, vol. 1/2e, Lettres et fragments, ed. J. Bidez (Paris: Collection des Universités de France, 1924) 85.6–9: Πηγάσιον...εἶναι δοκῶν τῶν Γαλιλαίων ἐπίσκοπος, ἠπίστατο σέβεσθαι καὶ τιμᾶν τοὺς θεούς.

20. Vlasios Pheidas, "The Church of Philippi in the First Three Centuries," Kavala and the Surrounding Area 2, 44.

21. Pelekanidis, "Kultprobleme im Apostel-Paulus Octogon," 2. 393–97.

pagan hero worship. An eloquent comment on the transition from paganism to Christianity was given by Pegasios, bishop of Troy, when he told Emperor Julian that the Trojans venerated the pagan heroes and the Christian martyrs equally because they were all honorable citizens of their city.[22] In other words, the transition from one religion to the other took place on a civic level.

André Grabar has pointed out that the octagonal forms in ecclesiastical buildings are related to mausoleums and martyria. This is manifest in the remains at Philippi, which indicate that the temple-shaped structure (fig. 7,3) with the underground Hellenistic tomb functioned continuously for some particular Christian cult throughout the use of the Octagon, until the late sixth or early seventh century.[23] Hundreds of early Christian small bronze coins (*minimi*) have been found inside the upper structure. They were the offerings of worshipers, demonstrating that the place was indeed used for worship.

Another installation at this site was also designated for worship.[24] A narrow passage east of the upper part of the heroon (fig. 7,4), containing a marble structure (fig. 7,5), was directly connected with the former. Pelekanidis describes this passage as a "diaconicon" with a "constructed table" (pl. XVI,1).[25] This constructed table consists of three marble slabs that, together with the eastern wall, comprise a rectangular, box-shaped container. Where these slabs connect to

---

22. Julian, *Lettres et fragments*, 85.5–6: "And why should it be strange that the Trojans venerate one of their honorable citizens as we worship the martyrs?" (Καὶ τί τοῦτο ἄτοπον, ἄνδρα ἀγαθὸν ἑαυτῶν πολίτην, ὥσπερ ἡμεῖς τοὺς μάρτυρας θεραπεύουσιν).

23. Bakirtzis, "The Day after the Destruction," 709.

24. Pelekanidis, *Praktika Archaeologikis Etaireias* (Athens) 1960, 88; Gounaris, *Balneum*, 55 n. 179.

25. Pelekanidis, *Praktika Archaeologikis Etaireias* (Athens) 1960, 90; Gounaris, *Balneum*, 51.

the wall and at their two corresponding exterior corners, sockets were carved, into which small columns were inserted. These columns supported a type of baldachin. Inside, salt and sediment deposits from prolonged water circulation are evident on the walls. The boxlike structure was covered by a horizontal marble slab fastened slightly lower than the lip of the walls, thus forming a shallow basin. On the top of the northern upright slab is an indentation for receiving a water-carrying pipe. At the bottom of the same slab is a hole for discharging the water. Through this hole, the water flowed into a circular cistern in the next room.

We now know that holy water flowed from this marble structure; for this reason Georgios Gounaris calls it a "holy-water cistern."[26] However, an examination of the hydraulic system through which plain water entered the structure from the balneum and emerged as holy water shows that the trans-mutation took place inside the marble structure itself. The holy water was then channeled into the small cistern in the adjacent room where it could be drawn by the faithful. Eustathios, the twelfth-century metropolitan of Thessalonike, attested that holy water flowed from sacred relics.[27] So if we accept that this marble structure in the Octagon, from which the holy water flowed, contained sacred relics, then it is clearly neither a table nor a holy-water cistern but must represent the sarcophagus of some holy person. Its shape supports this theory, and it even had a ciborium at one time, with columns at its two outer corners. Thus it served as a sarcophagus-cenotaph, a replica of the real tomb of the martyr, which was underground in the nearby vaulted tomb. The gushing forth of holy water from the martyr's

---

26. Gounaris, *Balneum,* 52.
27. Th. L. E. Tafel, *Eustathii metropolitae Thessalonicensis opuscula* (1832; reprint, Amsterdam: Adolf M. Hakkert, 1964) 171.

tomb brought the worshiper into contact with the martyr's gracious power.

This combination of one tomb above ground and another below was also seen in another great shrine, that of Saint Demetrios in Thessalonike, where, according to the "Miracles of St Demetrios," the saint's tomb was believed to lie beneath the *kline* that bore his effigy.[28] Whose tomb was this? Why not Saint Paul's? We have the inscriptional evidence that the church was dedicated to his memory. The legend that Paul was buried in Rome is a later one for which there is no historical evidence.[29] Furthermore, relics were often moved about in the early Christian and medieval periods, and it is very likely that the Apostolic Church of Philippi, which had such close links with Paul, possessed at least some of his relics. That the church represented Philippi's pride in its apostolic origins is evident in the text of a Justinian funerary mosaic inscription from Philippi: "...the city of Philipp of Macedon [Philippi], whose presiding Church (of Philippi), renowned for and proud of her apostolic links...."[30]

In place of the Christian assembly hall, which had been dedicated in memory of the apostle Paul and which dates to roughly 313–50 CE, a large church in the shape of an octagon with a shallow projecting apse at the eastern side was built in approximately 400 CE. In the middle of the fifth cen-

---

28. Paul Lemerle, *Les plus anciens recueils des miracles de Saint Démétrius,* vol. 1, *Le texte* (Paris: Éditions du Center National de la Recherche Scientifique, Le Monde Byzantin, 1979) 1/1. 22; 1/6. 55; 1/10. 88; for a comparison of the tomb at the Octagon in Philippi and the tomb of Saint Demetrios in Thessalonike, see Charalambos Bakirtzis, "Le culte de Saint Démétrius," *Akten des XII. Internationalen Kongress für christliche Archäologie, Bonn 22. bis 28. September 1991;* Jahrbuch für Antike und Christentum, Ergänzungsband 20,1 (1995) 58–68.

29. See Helmut Koester, chap. 3, in this volume.

30. Unpublished.

tury CE, niches were added in each of the four corners of
the church; thus the free octagon was changed into an octagon inscribed in a square. The apse of the chancel was
also lengthened. This type of church belongs to the traditional pattern of the Eastern centralized martyria, such as
the church of Mary Theotokos on Mt. Gerazim (484 CE) in
Palestine and the martyrium of Saint George at Ezra (also
called Zarah; 515 CE) in Syria. In my opinion all the archaeological and historical information together provides an
answer to the question of why an eight-sided church was
built on this particular site in Philippi.

We have no idea whether or not the tradition of Saint Paul
remained alive at Philippi thereafter, and it was not until
modern times that scholarly traditions revived the memory
of the "apostle of the nations" in Philippi. A frescoed underground chamber discovered in 1878 was taken to be the
"prison of St Paul" (pls. V,8; VIII,1);[31] and a marble bollard
from Neapolis harbor, now in the courtyard of the church of
Saint Nicholas in Kavala (pl. XVI,2), is popularly believed to
be the rostrum from which Saint Paul spoke. In the early seventh century CE, Philippi declined; its monumental buildings,
including the Octagon, collapsed; its population diminished,
and the once flourishing center of pilgrimage became no
more than a farming settlement.[32]

---

31. Lemerle, *Philippes,* 296; Elli Pelekanidou, "The Traditional Prison
of St. Paul in Philippi," *Kavala and the Surrounding Area 1,* 427–35. It is
not certain that the underground cistern, which today is known as "Saint
Paul's prison," is the frescoed underground chamber discovered in 1878
or that the few frescoes preserved there can be dated to the tenth century.

32. Bakirtzis, "The Day after the Destruction," 709.

3

PAUL AND PHILIPPI

The Evidence from Early Christian Literature

Helmut Koester

Philippi in 1 Thessalonians and in the Acts of the Apostles

Philippi is mentioned in the oldest writing of the New Testament, Paul's Letter to the Thessalonians, written from Corinth probably in the fall of the year 50 CE. The following events of the same year determine the context for the writing of this letter:[1] (1) In the spring, Paul had come from Troas to Philippi, where he had the opportunity to preach the gospel and to found a community. (2) After being forced to leave Philippi, Paul moved to Thessalonike, where he must have stayed several months. (3) From Thessalonike he traveled to Athens; from there he sent Timothy to Thessalonike (1 Thess 3:1–2). (4) Timothy returned to Paul with good news about the faith of the Thessalonians (1 Thess 3:6). (5) Paul writes to the Thessalonians.[2]

---

1. On the chronology of the events, see Bormann, *Philippi*, 118–26.

2. It is not clear whether the letter was written while Paul was still in Athens or after his arrival in Corinth. The subscriptions of the ancient manuscripts of 1 Thessalonians vary; A B 1 0278. 1739. 1881 and the majority of the manuscripts read πρὸς Θεσσαλονικεῖς α´ ἐγράφη ἀπὸ Ἀθηνῶν

While Paul is writing to the Thessalonians in detail about
his mission in their city and about his close relationship with
that community, he says nothing about the founding of a
community in Philippi. Rather, Paul and his associates state
simply that they were able to preach the gospel freely in
Thessalonike, "after they had previously suffered and been
shamefully treated in Philippi" (προπαθόντες καὶ ὑβρισθέντες
ἐν Φιλίπποις;[3] 1 Thess 2:2). We can obtain no other details
from the letters of Paul about this first visit. However, the letters to the Philippians, which Paul later wrote from Ephesos
(see pp. 52–58), leave no doubt that Paul did indeed establish
a community in Philippi during his first visit of the city; as far
as we know, he did not visit Philippi again before he wrote
those letters.[4] Moreover, according to Phil 4:15, the Philippians had supported Paul from the beginning of his missionary
work in Macedonia and Greece, and Phil 4:16 even states
that the Philippians sent some support to Paul during his
ministry in Thessalonike.[5]

Acts 16:11–40 presents a rather lengthy and detailed report about Paul's first visit to Philippi. Coming from Troas,
with a stop at Samothrake, Paul, Silas, and Timothy arrived
in Neapolis and went from there to Philippi. The city is correctly designated as a Roman colony (Acts 16:12). However,
the following statement about the relationship of Philippi to

---

(1739 *pc* add διὰ Τιμοθέου). 81 *pc* read πρὸς Θεσσαλονικεῖς α´ ἐγράφη ἀπὸ
Κορίνθου ὑπὸ Παύλου καὶ Σιλουανοῦ καὶ Τιμοθέου.

3. On the hapaxlegomenon προπάσχειν, see Beda Rigaux, *Saint Paul:
Les Épitres aux Thessaloniciens* (EBib; Paris: Gabalda, 1956) 401–2. The
προ- points to an event that happened at a preceding time.

4. According to Acts 18:18–20 he traveled to Ephesos directly from
Corinth and then returned to Ephesos after a visit in Caesarea and Antioch
(Acts 18:21–23).

5. It is also likely that the mention of "the brothers from Macedonia" (2 Cor 11:9) who came to Corinth with support for Paul, refers to
delegates from Philippi; see Bormann, *Philippi*, 122.

Macedonia is unclear. The best attested reading, "which is the leading city of the district of Macedonia" (ἥτις ἐστὶν πρώτη μερίδος τῆς Μακεδονίας πόλις),[6] is certainly wrong and cannot be ascribed to Luke, who had a good knowledge of locality and geography; neither was Philippi a capital nor Macedonia a "district." The best reading is the conjecture "which belongs to the first district of Macedonia" (ἥτις ἐστὶν πρώτης μερίδος τῆς Μακεδονίας πόλις).[7]

The report about the stay of Paul and his two fellow apostles in Philippi need not be discussed in full here. Acts 16:13–14 reports a meeting on the sabbath day with women, among them Lydia from Thyatira, who was soon baptized, at the river outside of the city gate at a "place of prayer" (προσευχή).[8] Then follows an episode of a slave girl who had a spirit of divination (πύθων) and the accusation of the apostles by the girl's owners because they had lost their source of income after Paul had exorcised her prophetic spirit. The result is an attack by the mob and the public beating of the three apostles, an imprisonment, an earthquake that opens the door of the jail, and the conversion and baptism of the jailer with his family. Finally, the release

6. 𝔓⁷⁴ ℵ A C Ψ 33. 36. 81. 323. 945. 1175. 1891 *pc.*
7. See Conzelmann, *Acts of the Apostles*, 129–31.
8. The Greek text is problematic here. It seems that the grammatically incorrect text of A and B (οὗ ἐνομίζομεν [𝔓⁴⁵ ἐνόμιζεν] προσευχὴ [*sic*] εἶναι) was the most original reading. "The variants can be explained in the simplest way if the original had an incorrect nominative (προσευχή) instead of the accusative (προσευχήν)" (Conzelmann, *Acts of the Apostles*, 130).
It is strange that Acts 16:13 says, "where we *supposed* that there was a place of prayer." One wonders, moreover, why only women were there. "Place of prayer" (προσευχή) can be used as a designation for a synagogue; see Shaye J. D. Cohen, *From the Maccabees to the Mishnah* (Library of Early Christianity; Philadelphia: Westminster, 1989) 111–12. On the inscription from Philippi that mentions a synagogue (συναγωγή), see Chaido Koukouli-Chrysantaki, pp. 28–35 in this volume.

of the apostles and their departure after another visit with
Lydia and other brothers and sisters are typical for Luke's
composition of the travel narrative.

There are a number of problems in this account from the
Book of Acts. Here, as elsewhere, Paul's stay is depicted as
rather short — quite unlikely if one considers the fact of the
founding of a new Christian community that remained unusu-
ally faithful to Paul during the following years of his mission.
The designation of the governors of the city as στρατηγοί,
which is the normal translation of *duumviri* (or *duoviri*), is
correct and reveals Luke's good knowledge of the local situation. The story of the exorcism belongs to the common stock
of stories about powerful deeds enacted by Christian miracle workers; compare *Ps.-Clem. Hom.* 9.16.3: "For pythons
prophesy (πύθωνες μαντεύονται), but they are cast out by us
as demons and put to flight." The miracle of the earthquake
is a response to the singing of hymns in prison — again a
motif that has its parallels elsewhere (cf. *Test. Jos.* 8.5). Legends formed early around the memory of the visits of famous
apostles. They may have been part of the local tradition at
the time of the writing of the Acts of the Apostles by Luke.

Paul and Philippi according to the Letter to the Philippians

Philippi is next mentioned in Paul's Letter to the Philippians.
It is my opinion that this letter of Paul, which is written from
prison, was not written from Rome but from Ephesos. The
question of the Ephesian imprisonment of Paul is complex
and cannot be discussed here.[9] To be sure, the ancient *sub-*

---

9. Since the fundamental work of Wilhelm Michaelis (*Die Gefangen-
schaft des Paulus in Ephesus und das Itinerar des Timotheus* [Gütersloh:

scriptio to this letter, which appears in the majority of the Byzantine manuscripts and in the Syriac translation, is probably quite old. It reads ἐγράφη ἀπὸ Ῥώμης δι᾽ Ἐπαφροδίτου. Since, however, Paul writes in this letter of his hope that he might live and return to the church (Phil 1:24), the subscription might rest on a tradition that Paul indeed did not die in Rome. Still, no certain conclusion can be drawn from this secondary addition to the letter.

Accepting the hypothesis of an Ephesian origin of the Letter to the Philippians renders a further consideration more plausible, namely, that this letter is a compilation of three letters by Paul to Philippi that were written from Ephesos.[10] The hypothesis of Ephesos as the place of the writing of Philippians and the hypothesis of the division of Philippians into three smaller letters support each other. A quick exchange of letters and messengers, which is clearly indicated in Philippians, is much more likely if Paul was imprisoned in Ephesos, not as far away as Rome; the long and arduous travel between Rome and Philippi would have prevented a speedy correspondence. If the Philippian letters were written from Ephesos, they must be dated in the winter of 54–55 CE — the most likely date for the Ephesian imprisonment of Paul,[11] that is, before 2 Corinthians 1:8ff., where Paul

---

Bertelsmann, 1925]), it has been widely agreed that the so-called Imprisonment Letters, at least Philippians and Philemon, must be dated at the time of an Ephesian imprisonment of the apostle. See especially G. S. Duncan, *Paul's Ephesian Ministry: A Reconstruction with Special Reference to the Ephesian Origin of the Imprisonment Epistles* (New York: Scribner, 1929); T. W. Manson, "St. Paul in Ephesus: The Date of the Epistle to the Philippians," *Bulletin of the John Rylands Library* 23 (1958/59) 43–45.

10. A detailed discussion of the various division hypotheses of the Epistle to the Philippians has been presented by Bormann, *Philippi*, 108–18.

11. See Helmut Koester, *Introduction to the New Testament*, vol. 2, *History and Literature of Early Christianity* (Philadelphia: Fortress; Berlin and New York: de Gruyter, 1982) 103–4, 130–32.

speaks of the suffering and the threat of death that had been hanging over him during his stay in Ephesos.

While Paul was in prison, he received a gift from the church in Philippi, and he acknowledged this gift in Phil 4:10–20,[12] the first of the three letters that are now combined into the extant writing to the Philippians.[13] Epaphroditos came to Paul from Philippi as the bearer of the gift (4:18). This short letter — its genre is a formal receipt[14] — contains significant information about Paul's relationship to the Philippian church: the Philippians had already supported Paul at the beginning of his ministry in Macedonia by sending support to Thessalonike (Phil 4:15–16), and while then they did not have an opportunity (ἠκαιρεῖσθε) to show their concern for Paul for some time, they have now once more come to his aid (4:10).

The second letter,[15] comprising Philippians 1:1–3:1,[16] must have been written somewhat later. Some time must have passed; the Philippians had heard meanwhile that Epaphroditos had fallen sick (Phil 2:26b). While Phil 4:18 simply mentioned Epaphroditos as the bringer of the gift,

---

12. Probably also 4:21–23 belongs to this letter, unless these verses are the conclusion of the second letter, Phil 1:1–3:1.

13. A detailed explanation of this letter and of the problems of its interpretation is given by Bormann, *Philippi*, 136–60.

14. Phil 4:18 uses the traditional formula for the acknowledgment of such a gift: "I have been paid in full and I have more than enough; I am fully satisfied, now that I received from Epaphroditus the gifts you sent" (NRSV).

15. That the transition from 3:1 to 3:2 is very harsh has been observed often. While Phil 3:1 emphasizes the joy that Paul has in the Lord, Phil 3:2 begins abruptly with a stern warning. It is difficult to reconcile these two statements as part of one and the same letter.

16. It is debated whether also Phil 4:2–7, 8–9, and 21–23 should be assigned to this second letter. The latest investigation of this problem by Bormann (*Philippi*, 115–18) assigns 4:2–7 to the second letter, while 4:8–9 are seen as a part of the third letter (Phil 3:2–4:1).

Paul now reports that Epaphroditos had stayed with him and had not only served him on behalf of the Philippians (2:30)[17] but had also become sick: "Indeed he was so ill that he nearly died" (2:27a). However, he was now well again, and Paul wants to send him to Philippi soon (2:27b–28).

It is possible that the mission of Epaphroditos on behalf of the Philippians involved more than just the transfer of a sum of money. This possibility has been explored recently by Lukas Bormann,[18] especially in the context of the mention of "those from the household of Caesar" (οἱ ἐκ τῆς Καίσαρος οἰκίας) in Phil 4:22 and of the reference to the "imperial guard" (πραιτώριον) — the official residence of the proconsul, where the trial of Paul was taking place and where also the gospel of Christ had become known (Phil 1:13). Philippi was a Roman colony. It is possible that Epaphroditus, a citizen of this colony, was sent to Ephesos because he may have had special connections to freedmen of the *praetorium* — a very influential group especially at the time of Claudius and Nero — and could therefore influence the outcome of Paul's trial.

It is evident that Paul, when he wrote this second letter to the Philippians, was more optimistic about a positive outcome to his trial. He wants to send Timothy to Philippi as soon as possible (Phil 2:19), and should he receive a favorable sentence, he himself would go to Philippi in the near future (1:26; 2:24). This intention fits with Paul's travel plans as they are known from the Corinthian correspondence, where Paul mentions his plan to visit Corinth by way of Macedonia (1 Cor 16:5) — and this is precisely what Paul did after he left Ephesos following his release from prison.[19]

---

17. "...risking his life to make up for those services that you could not provide for me."

18. See the discussion in Bormann, *Philippi*, 213–17 and passim.

19. The letter preserved in 2 Cor 1:1–2:13 and 7:5–15 must have been

A fragment of a third letter of uncertain date is preserved in Phil 3:2–4:1.[20] This letter does not reflect anything about Paul's imprisonment. However, since it is only a fragment, it is impossible to tell what was said in the letter's proem and greetings. This third letter is a stern warning against a group of Judaizing apostles who had come to Philippi for their own perfectionist propaganda — perhaps the same group that already had caused trouble for Paul in Galatia. However, the problem of these opponents can be left aside here.[21]

If the hypothesis is correct that the extant letter of Paul to the Philippians is a composition of three letters from Paul, it is necessary to ask why the preserved document was edited in this fashion, presumably by the church of the Philippians before or during the process of the first collection of the letters of Paul,[22] some time during the final decades of the first century CE.[23] Of the three original letters, the second letter, which emphasizes the imprisonment and impending death of Paul most strongly, has been used as the beginning for the edition by the Philippian church. From this letter, the editor drew the prescript and proem (1:1–2 and 1:2–11) as well

---

written from Macedonia, perhaps from Philippi. On the division hypothesis of 2 Corinthians, see Dieter Georgi, *The Opponents of Paul in Second Corinthians* (Philadelphia: Fortress, 1986) 9–18. Also the two letters concerning the collection for Jerusalem, 2 Corinthians 8 and 2 Corinthians 9, must have been written from here; see especially 2 Cor 9:4.

20. Perhaps also 4:8–9 must be assigned to this letter; see Bormann, *Philippi*, 118 and the discussion on the preceding pages of his book.

21. See Helmut Koester, "The Purpose of the Polemic of a Pauline Fragment (Philippians III)," *NTS* 8 (1961/62) 317–32.

22. It is quite possible that a knowledge of several letters from Paul to the Philippians is presupposed in Polycarp of Smyrna, who reminds the Philippians in his letter to that church (3.2) that Paul had written letters to them (ὑμῖν ἔγραψεν ἐπιστολάς).

23. Bormann, *Philippi*, 128–36, discusses several hypotheses about the composition of the three letters into one and concludes that the Philippians themselves were responsible for the one-letter edition.

as most of the corpus of the letter (1:12–3:1). The greeting of this letter has disappeared, while the greetings of the first letter serve as the conclusion for the new edition. The proem of this second letter is dominated by the concept of martyrdom. It is in these verses that Paul emphasizes that the Philippians are fellows (κοινωνία, συγκοινωνοί) of his suffering as well as of the proclamation of the gospel. In the following body of this second letter, it is again the possibility of Paul's death that dominates. It would be a gain if Paul were dying and were with Christ (1:19ff), and after the quotation of the famous "Christ hymn" in Phil 2:5–11, Paul once more emphasizes that he is already spent as an offering for Christ in the service of the church (2:17). At the same time, the first letter (4:10–23), which describes the financial relations between Paul and the Philippians, is relegated to an insignificant position at the end. This is surprising because the Philippians could have chosen to set a memorial for themselves[24] as a church that had supported Paul financially in his ministry.

The church of Philippi, sometime at the end of the first century, edited these fragments of Paul's letters to their church in such a way that the concept of Paul's martyrdom was most prominently tied to this particular correspondence. Is it possible to assume that already at this time the Philippian church claimed a special relationship to the martyrdom and death of the apostle? Is the edition of the extant letter a testimony to the death of Paul in Philippi? If one cannot answer these questions definitively in the affirmative, still the possibility that the composition of the letter in its extant

---

24. Günther Bornkamm ("Der Philipperbrief als paulinische Briefsammlung," in *Geschichte und Glaube II = Gesammelte Aufsätze 4* [BEvT 53; Munich: Kaiser, 1971] 203), commenting on the position of the first letter at the end, speaks about the intention of the Philippians to establish a nice memorial ("ein schönes Denkmal") for themselves.

form was prompted by Philippi's claim to the martyrdom of Paul cannot be excluded.

The city of Philippi is mentioned once more in the Book of Acts in 20:6, where Paul sailed "out of Philippi" for Troas after the Feast of the Unleavened Breads, when he was heading for Jerusalem by way of Corinth. But it is certain that Paul had already come through Philippi once before. In 2 Cor 1:15–16; 2:12–13, and 7:5, Paul reports that after his release from imprisonment in Ephesos, he went from Troas through Macedonia to Corinth, expecting to meet Titus, whom he had sent ahead to Corinth. Thus he must have come through Macedonia twice: first in the fall of the year 55 on his way to Corinth, where he stayed through the winter, and then in the spring of the year 56 on his journey to Jerusalem as reported by Acts 20:6.

The Conclusion of the Book of Acts

There are no further references to Philippi in the New Testament either in the Book of Acts or in any of the deutero-Pauline writings. But neither is there any mention of the martyrdom of Paul in Rome or in any other place. This seems strange. To be sure, it would have been counterproductive for the author of the Book of Acts to say anything about Paul after his arrival in Rome because the purpose of Acts is to show the triumphal progress of the gospel of Christ from Jerusalem, the ancient capital of Israel, to Rome, the capital of the Roman Empire. Thus its ending with the description of Paul's successful and "unhindered" preaching in Rome for a period of two years would seem an adequate conclusion to the book.

A number of hypotheses have been proposed in order to

explain why Luke does not report the martyrdom of Paul in Rome at the end of his work:[25]

1. Luke intended to write a third volume. As it stands now, however, the work is a complete entity that fulfills the explicit purpose of the author's plan, namely, to present the two epochs of salvation history, the time of the revelation in Jesus' ministry and the time of the church.

2. Luke wrote and completed his work before the trial of Paul had begun. This hypothesis assumes a very early date for the composition of Luke's work, which cannot be confirmed by other observations — a date at the end of the century is much more likely.

3. Paul's martyrdom was originally part of the book but has been removed or otherwise lost; yet, there is no sign that the conclusion of the book is fragmentary.

4. Paul was not martyred then at all; rather the case was dismissed after a two-year period had expired. His martyrdom took place a few years later, perhaps at the occasion of the well-attested persecution of the Christians in Rome after Nero himself had been accused of setting the fire that destroyed a large part of the city.

Paul's Place of Martyrdom in the Pastoral Epistles

Perhaps it is possible to suggest another version of this fourth hypothesis: Luke knew that Paul was not martyred in Rome

---

25. See the summary of these hypotheses and relevant literature in Conzelmann, *Acts of the Apostles,* and Ernst Haenchen, *The Acts of the Apostles: A Commentary* (Philadelphia: Westminster, 1971), on Acts 28:30–31.

at all but later returned to the East, where he eventually found his death as a martyr. The New Testament itself does not report such a martyrdom in the East, nor at any other place, and there is no positive indication for such a return to the East. Nonetheless, a few related puzzles are left in the deutero-Pauline epistles, to wit, in the Pastoral Epistles, 1 and 2 Timothy and Titus. To be sure, these letters are certainly not written by Paul. Most critical scholars assume a date for their composition between the end of the first century and the middle of the second.[26] What is the situation that these letters presuppose?[27]

1 Tim 1:3 says, "I commanded you to remain in Ephesos, when I traveled to Macedonia." This situation is difficult to fit into Paul's travels as they are known from the Book of Acts and from Paul's genuine epistles. On his first trip to Macedonia, Paul was not alone. According to Acts 16:1ff, Timothy was with Paul, and Paul had not even been to Ephesos yet. In Acts 20:1, the apostle had sent Timothy from Ephesos ahead of him with the intention to meet him again in Macedonia (Acts 19:22; this agrees with Phil 2:19). It is

---

26. For the question of the date and authenticity of the Pastoral Epistles, see Martin Dibelius and Hans Conzelmann, *The Pastoral Epistles: A Commentary on the Pastoral Epistles* (Hermeneia; Philadelphia: Fortress, 1972) 1–5.

27. The situations of the Pastoral Epistles and the question of whether these situations rely on any historical information have been discussed repeatedly; see Dibelius and Conzelmann, *The Pastoral Epistles,* 15–16, 126–28, 152–54. It is doubtful whether the subscriptions of ancient manuscripts are of any help in informing us about Paul's assumed place of authorship. For 1 Timothy, they suggest Nikopolis of Laodikeia in Phrygia; for 2 Timothy, almost all manuscripts designate Rome as the place of composition (except for Codex A, which gives Laodikeia); for the composition of the Letter to Titus, ancient manuscripts list Nikopolis, Macedonia, or Neapolis in Macedonia. However, it is interesting that the manuscript tradition is not unanimous for Rome as the place at which the Pastoral Epistles were composed.

therefore not possible to fit the situation of 1 Tim 1:2–3 into the Pauline itinerary as it is known from the Book of Acts as well as from Paul's genuine letters. Thus the situation of 1 Tim 1:3 assumes a stay by Paul in the East after his Roman imprisonment. If Paul was martyred in Rome, one would have to assume that this martyrdom did not take place at the Roman imprisonment reported by Acts 28 but during a second Roman imprisonment that took place after another visit by Paul to Asia Minor, Macedonia, and Greece.

In the last of the Pastoral Epistles, the Letter to Titus, Paul is somewhere in Greece, planning to spend the winter in Nikopolis (most likely Nikopolis in Epirus, then the most important city of western Greece; Titus 3:12). Such a winter stay again does not fit into the locations known from either the Book of Acts or the genuine Pauline letters. It must therefore be dated to a later journey of Paul's after his Roman imprisonment.

The situation of 2 Timothy is more difficult to understand. Here, Paul is certainly imprisoned and expects possible martyrdom (2 Tim 1:17; 4:16–17; also 4:6–8). But it is unlikely that this refers to a second imprisonment in Rome. Some scholars have speculated that the letter refers to the Caesarean imprisonment,[28] but this is very unlikely. The various instructions to Timothy, who is in Ephesos, imply rather that Paul is somewhere in the area of Greece or Macedonia: "Make every effort to come to me quickly" (2 Tim 4:9); "Demas...has gone to Thessalonike, Crescens to Galatia, Titus to Dalmatia" (4:10); "Tychikus I have sent to Ephesos" (4:12); "Erastus remained in Corinth. I had to leave Trophimus behind in Miletus" (4:20); "When you come, bring the coat I left in Troas with Carpus" (4:13). Philippi

---

28. P. N. Harrison, *The Problem of the Pastoral Epistles* (London: Oxford University Press, 1921) 121ff.

is not an impossible place for such a final imprisonment of Paul. If Timothy is coming from Ephesos to Paul in Philippi, Troas, where Paul left his coat, is on the way.

I would reconstruct the assumed situations of Paul in the Pastoral Epistles as follows. After the Roman imprisonment (and missionary activity in Spain?), Paul returned to the East and went to Crete together with Titus. Returning from there to Greece, he intended to spend the winter in Nikopolis and wrote to Titus to join him there. Thus the Epistle to Titus is the first of these three letters. Writing 1 Timothy, Paul is in Macedonia and writes to Timothy in Ephesos. Neither Titus nor 1 Timothy indicates that Paul is in prison. However, at the writing of 2 Timothy, Paul is indeed imprisoned and has just passed through the first part of his trial. Since Paul is writing to Timothy with the request that Timothy come to him and bring a number of things that Paul left in Troas, the place assumed for this writing is most likely a city of Macedonia, perhaps Philippi.

These pieces of personal information about Paul and of the various instructions are either fragments from genuine Pauline letters, which have been used for the composition of the Pastoral Epistles,[29] or they are fictitious. In the first case, they would represent evidence that Paul indeed returned from Rome after the imprisonment mentioned at the end of the Book of Acts; they would indicate that Paul's martyrdom must have taken place in a city of Macedonia. In the second case, that is, if the information is fictitious, these pieces of personal information reveal that the author of the Pastoral Epistles knew of a tradition that claimed a period of Paul's return to the East and martyrdom there, to

---

29. That there were genuine letters written by Paul that have not been included in the later collection of the letters of the Pauline corpus is evident from 1 Cor 5:9, where Paul mentions an earlier letter that he had written to Corinth before the writing of 1 Corinthians.

wit, in Philippi.[30] In either case, neither the Pastoral Epistles nor any other New Testament writings say anything about a Roman martyrdom of Paul. All information gathered from the books of the New Testament canon would not conflict with the assumption that Paul was martyred in Philippi.

The *Acts of Paul* and the Martyrdom of Paul in Rome

What then is the origin of the information about Paul's martyrdom in Rome? The entire early Christian literature to the middle or even late second century CE knows nothing about a Roman martyrdom of Paul. The apostolic fathers presuppose the martyrdom of Paul. But neither *1 Clem.* 5.5 nor Ign. *Rom.* 4.3 says anything about the place of this martyrdom. The earliest information about the Roman martyrdom of Paul comes from the *Acts of Paul,* which was written in the last decades of the second century CE.[31] In this book, Paul comes from Corinth to Italy. When he is still on the ship, Christ appears to Paul and reveals that he has to be crucified again.[32] The recounting of this episode especially raises the question of whether the author of the *Acts of Paul* possessed any genuine information or sources for his story because there can be no question that this episode was borrowed from the *Acts of Peter.*[33] Moreover, for the brief description of Paul's activity in Rome, the author reports the

---

30. It must also be mentioned here that the pseudepigraphical correspondence known as *3 Corinthians,* preserved in the apocryphal *Acts of Paul,* locates the imprisoned apostle in Philippi.

31. See Wilhelm Schneemelcher, "Acts of Paul," in *New Testament Apocrypha,* 2. 213–37.

32. Ibid., 258.

33. Ibid., 314. The episode is original in the *Acts of Peter* because it serves as a prediction of Peter's crucifixion. In the *Acts of Paul,* it makes

episode of the cupbearer of Caesar Patroklos who fell from a window and died in his attempt to hear Paul,[34] a story the author has simply borrowed from Acts 20:9–12. This demonstrates that the author had no materials that could help him to find a cause for Paul's imprisonment, trial, and execution. Everything is invented here, and it is clear that the author of the *Acts of Paul* could not rely on any older report of Paul's martyrdom. He probably did not know anything else but the claim of the Roman church that she occupied the place at which the great apostle was martyred.

That Rome indeed claimed at the end of the second century to be the place of the martyrdom of both Peter and Paul is evident from several authors quoted by Eusebius. However, one of these quotations, namely, a sentence from the Epistle to the Romans by Bishop Dionysios of Corinth (ca. 170), does not explicitly mention Rome as the place of Paul's martyrdom:

> By so great an admonition you bound together the foundations of the Romans and Corinthians by Peter and Paul, for both of them taught together in our Corinth and were our founders, and together also taught in Italy in the same place and were martyred at the same time. (*Hist. eccl.* 2.25.8).[35]

It must be noted that the reference to the martyrdom of both apostles has as little historical value as the information that Peter and Paul taught together in Corinth, which is evidently false. Moreover, Dionysios does not say that both apostles were martyred "at the same place" but "at the same time" (κατὰ τὸν αὐτὸν καιρόν).

---

little sense because the author continues to tell that Paul was not crucified but beheaded.

34. Ibid., 261.

35. Translation by Kirsopp Lake in LCL, 2. 182–83.

Just before the quotation from Dionysios's letter, Eusebius quotes the Antimontanist writer Caius, who wrote against Montanus's successor Proclus at the time of the Roman bishop Zephyrinus (198–217):

> But I can point out the trophies of the apostles (τὰ τροπαία τῶν ἀποστόλων), for if you will go to the Vatican or to the Ostian Way, you will find the trophies of those who founded this church. (*Hist. eccl.* 2.25.7)[36]

Caius does not mention any of these founding apostles by name, but Eusebius may be right in inferring that he was speaking about Peter and Paul.

Eusebius still adduces another witness, namely, a remark in Origen's commentary on Genesis, although he does not provide an explicit quotation:

> What need be said of Paul, who fulfilled the gospel of Christ from Jerusalem to Illyria and afterward was martyred in Rome under Nero? This is stated exactly by Origen in the third volume of his commentary on Genesis. (*Hist. eccl.* 3.1.3)[37]

This reference shows that the Roman claim to be the place of the martyrdom of Paul was also known in the East in the beginning of the third century. This does not exclude, however, the possibility that another church, namely, Philippi, may have made a similar claim. That this was indeed the case could be concluded from the recent excavations of the Octagonal Church complex in Philippi.

---

36. Ibid.
37. Ibid., 2. 190–91.

4

DEAD PAUL

The Apostle as Martyr in Philippi

Allen Dwight Callahan

Our point of departure, and the point of departure for the various extracanonical traditions about Paul, is the Pauline corpus and the Acts of the Apostles, which together provide us with a composite sketch of the canonical Paul. Or, rather than a sketch, a better metaphor to describe these materials is that of a pastiche. The Paul of the New Testament is a pastiche made up of epistolary and narrative pieces, placed together by ecclesiastical tradition and modern scholarship. They have been placed end to end in a collection of letters to different people from different times and places throughout the apostle's troubled career. Modern Western scholarship has claimed that several of these letters, our only link to the apostle's *ipsissima vox,* are not Paul's at all, but the creations of imitators, admirers, and amanuenses of the apostle, writing in his name and after his death. Though attribution of these letters is disputed, it is clear that other admirers, even more obscure, later gathered these pieces together; they not only preserved these letters but trimmed the pieces to fit into their new setting as a collection. The result was a monumental theological achievement: a new totality of Christian literary artifacts thus came into being, the whole being far greater in its theological and ecclesiastical impact than the sum of its parts. These editors are the unknown artists to whom we must give credit for our present epistolary pastiche.

Yet for some ancient readers, this body of Pauline letters was not fitly joined together. Lacunae in the corpus itself called for its supplementation. The *Epistle to the Laodiceans,* included in the collection of Paul's letters found in the New Testament of the Latin Vulgate, is itself a pastiche, made up of snippets from several of the canonical letters as well as other parts of the New Testament, but mostly from Paul's letter to the Philippians. Its fabricator, or fabricators, probably intended it to be read as the letter mentioned in Col 4:16. It is thus a purely literary creation and promises to tell us little about Paul or even what the early church thought of him. The very existence of the *Epistle to the Laodiceans,* however, shows that some early readers of Paul's letters considered the Pauline corpus to be deficient without it. Just as the *Epistle to the Laodiceans* was added to the Latin version of the Pauline corpus, so the early Syrian version of the New Testament adopted *3 Corinthians* into its canon. Though *3 Corinthians* is found in the *Acts of Paul,* to which I shall turn shortly, it was nevertheless regarded as Pauline in its own right and apparently had a transmission history independent of the apocryphal *Acts.* The Syrian father Ephraim even wrote a commentary on the letter. This epistle is an amalgam of Pauline theologoumena and antignostic polemic that reflects the spirit of the canonical Corinthian correspondence only superficially, if at all.

The Gnostics also added members to the *corpus Paulinum.* In addition to their assiduous and complex exegesis of Paul's letters, advocates of Christian gnosis cited Paul as an authority for their revelatory experience. Three works in the cache of Coptic documents found at Nag Hammadi lay claim to the Pauline legacy. The *Hypostasis of the Archons* opens with the words and in the authority of Paul:

> On account of the reality (*hypostasis*) of the authorities (*eksousiai*), (inspired) by the spirit of the father of truth, the great apostle... referring to the "authorities of the darkness" (Col 1:13) — told us that "our contest is not against flesh and [blood]: rather the authorities of the universe and the spirits of wickedness (Eph 6:12).[1]

Here, Paul's gnostic vocabulary of principalities and powers, carnal and spiritual, blindness and light, are impressed into the narrative remythologization of the creation account in Genesis. This language also laces the *Prayer of Paul*[2] found in the Jung Codex. Just as the *Hypostasis of the Archons* is a gnostic rereading of Genesis, so the *Prayer* is in the genre of the Psalms but expressed in the Pauline idiom of grace and mystery. *The Apocalypse of Paul* in Nag Hammadi Codex V[3] apparently takes its cue from Paul's report of revelatory experience in 2 Corinthians 12:2–4. Irenaeus knows of a gnostic tradition of interpreting this experience.[4] This work, too, has ransacked the Pauline corpus for its vocabulary of revelation and supplements the apocalyptic ecstasy to which Paul obliquely lays claim in 2 Corinthians. Characteristically, creative gnostic interpretation has gone beyond the apostle's stated reticence in his letter. Though this *Apocalypse* is certainly not the apocryphal, non-gnostic *Apocalypse of Paul*[5]

---

1. *Hypostasis of the Archons,* in Robinson, *Nag Hammadi,* 162.
2. *Prayer of Paul,* in Robinson, *Nag Hammadi,* 27–28.
3. *Apocalypse of Paul,* in Robinson, *Nag Hammadi,* 256–59.
4. *Adv. haer.* 2.30.7.
5. Hugo Duensing and Aurelio de Santos Otero, *Apocalypse of Paul,* in Edgar Hennecke, *New Testament Apocrypha* (2 vols.; 3d ed. by Wilhelm Schneemelcher, trans. R. McL. Wilson; Philadelphia: Westmin-

known to the early Byzantine church historian Sozomen[6] and Augustine,[7] it is equally certain that the raison d'être of both the Gnostic apocalypse ascribed to Paul and the apocryphal apocalypse of Patristic vintage is to reveal the revelation that is concealed by Paul in 2 Corinthians.

If imitation is indeed the sincerest form of flattery, the canonical Pauline corpus has received lavish praise from Late Antiquity and the early medieval period. Not only were individual apocryphal letters fashioned under Paul's name, but the corpus as a collection was also imitated. The genteel, urbane correspondence of Paul and Seneca is a third-century CE corpus of apocryphal letters known to Augustine[8] and mentioned with admiration by Jerome,[9] who apparently regarded them as genuine. In this correspondence Paul, the great Christian apostle, and Seneca, the great Stoic philosopher, are represented as kindred spirits. They are both men of irreproachable piety, each recognizing the commitment of the other to the sublimest virtues. By implication, Pauline Christianity is shown to be in continuity with the best of Roman Stoic morality.

Though the Senecan correspondence is completely devoid of historical veracity, Seneca's prestige in medieval Western Christendom was nevertheless considerable. He is quoted as if a Patristic authority at the tenth council of Tours in 567 CE and is featured with Paul and Peter in a traditional Spanish marionette Passion play of the Middle Ages. That Seneca had

---

ster, 1963) 2. 712–48. For the abridged Greek text, see Constantinus von Tischendorf, "Apocalypsis Pauli," in idem, ed., *Apocalypses Apocryphae, Mosis, Esdrae, Pauli, Johannis, item Mariae Dormito: Additis Evangeliorum et Actuum Apocryphorum Supplementis* (Lipsiae: Herm. Mendelssohn, 1866) 34–69.

   6. *Hist. eccl.* 7.19.
   7. *In Evang. Iohan.* 98.8.
   8. *Ep.* 153.
   9. *De vir. ill.* 12.

ever met, let alone corresponded with, any of the apostles of course remains out of the question; thus the Senecan corpus holds no promise of historical information about Paul.

The New Testament has also placed beside its Pauline epistolary collection a repository of narratives about Paul in the Acts of the Apostles. The genre of the preserved traditions, that of historical narrative, or *diegesis,* has provided us with a unified, coherent picture of the apostle, but its very unity and coherence are problematic for our modern, hermeneutically suspicious readings. Luke's picture of Paul is at variance with what we might expect from the letters. In Acts 9, 22, and 26, the Lukan Paul recounts his encounter with the Risen Lord on the road to Damascus. But when Paul speaks of Jesus' special revelation to him in Galatians 1:15, 1 Corinthians 9:1, and Romans 15:16, the features of Luke's dramatic narrative are completely absent. In Acts 9:26, Paul departs Damascus for Jerusalem, where he is introduced to the apostles by Barnabas. In Galatians 1:17, however, Paul insists that he did not confer with the Jerusalem apostles until much later in his ministry. Whereas in Galatians 1 and 2, Paul stridently disavows his links to the apostolic circle in Judea, he is depicted in Acts 15 as a respectful collaborator with the Jerusalem leadership. And though Acts depicts Paul as having been chased out of Damascus by the Jews, Paul writes in 2 Corinthians 11:32 that it was the threats of the Nabatean king Aretas that caused him to beat a hasty retreat through a window in the city wall. In another discrepancy concerning the motive forces behind Paul's itinerations, Luke would have us believe that the "spirit of Jesus" impedes Paul's travel plans, yet the apostle himself writes in 1 Thessalonians 2:18 that the hindrance was not the Lord but Satan. According to Acts, Paul's habit was to preach first in synagogues and to turn to Gentile audiences only after being rejected by synagogue leaders. This modus operandi is described in Pisidian Antioch (Acts 13) and repeated in Iconium (Acts 14), Thessalonike, Beroia, and Athens (Acts 17), Corinth and Ephesos (Acts 18 and 19), and Rome (Acts 28). In Paul's letters we hear of none of this; the very word "synagogue" is not in his vocabulary. Paul understands himself first and foremost as apostle to the Gentiles, leaving Peter to preach to the Jews — a division of labor upon which he insists repeatedly in his correspondence (Gal 2:7; Rom 1:5; 15:16; etc.). Yet in the story of his providential visit to the Roman centurion Cornelius in Acts 10 and 11, it is Peter, not Paul, who undertakes the first Gentile mission, albeit under protest. We find in Galatians a vituperative condemnation of circumcision, yet in Acts 16 Paul himself directs his junior associate Timothy to submit to that painful rite. The inconsistences between the Lukan portrait of Paul and Paul's self-presentation in his letters are thus many and varied.

Yet at a profounder level, the letters and the Acts of the Apostles agree on the ultimate significance of Paul's ministry. It is Paul who brings the early Christian movement into the world of the imperial cities and merchant classes. Paul remains quintessentially the apostle to the Gentiles. Paul, more than any other early Christian figure, was associated with the transition of the early Christian movement from the Palestinian farmlands and fishing villages to the mainstream of life and the norms of Roman imperial culture. The stresses and strains of this adaptation can be seen in the New Testament itself, with Paul playing a central role in its attendant controversies. The book of Acts reflects a subsequent, and in some cases self-conscious, stages in this development and carries on the process of translating earliest Christianity geographically, culturally, and psychically from agrarian Palestine to urban Asia Minor and Europe. Luke, the first to fully narrativize Paul, is a literary champion of this relocation, and it is he who has contributed more by sheer volume to the New

Testament canon than any other early Christian author: he provided its third and longest Gospel and its longest single work, the Acts of the Apostles.

Luke presents Paul as the great harbinger of Christianity's northwestern expansion and the theological adjustments that make it possible; he disprivileges ancestral Israelite covenantal proscriptions while privileging Israelite monotheism, challenges Judaism's exclusivity while universalizing its claims to election, and disavows Jewish nationalism (and its potential for political violence) while cultivating a polite dialogue with Roman political authorities. In short, Paul embraces everything that the Greeks and Romans admired about Judaism and dispenses with those things they despised.

On these points Luke, the editors of the *corpus Paulinum*, the litterateurs of Nag Hammadi, the authors of the Pauline apocrypha, and even the Jewish-Christian enemies of the Pauline gospel mentioned by Irenaeus,[10] Origen,[11] and Eusebius[12] all agree with a concord deeper than chronology or theology. Paul is the champion of Gentile Christianity and the pioneer of Christian existence beyond the law and the land of Israel; on these points the canonical Paul, Luke, and the other early Christian reinventors of Paul agree. Paul's apocryphal correspondence reflects the contents of the canonical *corpus Paulinum,* and these contents are further conflated with other early Christian literature in a way that presupposes the emerging Christian canon of the New Testament. The importance of connections to the ancient Israelite religious heritage — sabbath observance, dietary laws, the legitimacy and integrity of Israel's ancestral theocracy,

---

10. *Adv. haer.* 1.26.2; 3.15.1.
11. *Contra Cels.* 5.65.
12. *Hist. eccl.* 3.27.4 et al.

circumcision — fade away as Paul is pressed further and
further into a Gentile world: names, places, customs, and
concerns are not Palestinian but Greek, Roman, and Asian.
The Lukan itinerary has provided the narrative paradigm for
Paul's permanent departure from Judaism.

But whereas the canonical and apocryphal materials con-
cur fundamentally on the significance of Paul's life, they
differ just as fundamentally on the significance of his death.
Paul and Luke agree with one another and against the
apocryphal *Acts* and other later witnesses that, for all his
hardships and privations, the canonical Paul is not a martyr. Luke ends his account of Paul's ministry in Acts with
Paul under a congenial house arrest. Luke's account of Paul's
Roman imprisonment in Acts 28:17–30 is comprised mostly
of discourse (vss. 17b–22, 25b–29) with only perfunctory
narration (vss. 17a, 23–25a, 30). This high ratio of discourse to narration indicates that, as with other discourses
in Acts, this account is primarily a Lukan composition. We
may therefore conclude that Luke had little or no traditional
material with which to work when composing his report
of Paul's incarceration in Rome. It is hard to imagine that
such traditional material would have been unknown to early
Christian communities in touch with the Roman church, and
so we may deduce from Luke's creativity that such traditions
may not have existed.

But we can say more in a summary way about the dearth
of Luke's traditional material and how creatively he used
what materials he may have had. Luke's interests apparently
were not served by martyrdom materials, and where Luke's
source or sources may have recorded the death of one of his
main characters, strange things happen in his narrative. The
martyrdom of Stephen at the hands of Jewish executioners is
highlighted by Luke in Acts 7 as a prime example of Jewish
treachery, a leitmotif of Acts. Some modern commentators

have recognized, however, that Acts 7 shows redactional seams that indicate Luke's rehabilitation of what was essentially a lynching narrative. Luke has refashioned an account of vigilante justice by impressing upon it the trappings of due process as an indictment of the Jewish leadership in Jerusalem. He has plied considerable redactional skill in exploiting another opportunity to incriminate Jewish authorities.

In the case of Acts 12, however, some observers have noted that the narrative of the apostles' arrest and incarceration reads much like a prelude to a martyr's death, Luke's triumphalist redaction notwithstanding. Peter's departure is especially curious when we consider that Acts 12 begins with a report of the martyrdom of the apostle James, which Luke laconically recounts without fanfare (12:2). Mention of James's death serves only as an introduction to the story of Peter's imprisonment, Luke's real interest. C. F. Nesbitt has suggested that the account of Peter's escape in Acts 12 is to be understood as a martyrdom account and that the apostle's departure to "another place" in vs. 17 is a circumlocution for death.[13] Nesbitt's theory has not gained wide acceptance, but Oscar Cullmann, though dubious, nevertheless concedes that it is "worthy of serious consideration."[14] Luke is loathe to be the bearer of such bad tidings, even though they may have been borne in his sources. Besides, Luke requests the pleasure of Peter's presence at the Jerusalem Council meeting to be recounted in chapter 15: any account of Peter's death preceding the council would therefore constitute major problems for Luke's narrative. Perhaps Luke's source actually reported the death of Peter as a consequence of his imprisonment, and Luke suppressed this report

---

13. C. F. Nesbitt, "What Did Become of Peter?" *JBR* 27 (1959) 10–16.

14. Oscar Cullmann, *Peter: Disciple-Apostle-Martyr* (Philadelphia: Westminster, 1953) 38.

with the same freedom that allowed him to all but dismiss
the death of James.

The other incarceration account of Acts, that of the Philippian imprisonment of Paul and Silas in Acts 16, also presents
symptoms of a rehabilitated martyrdom account. Legendary
features abound side by side with travel notices using the first
person plural, perhaps a vestige of one of Luke's sources. The
miraculous jailbreak of vss. 25–34 is Luke's own narrative
intervention. Whereas sources of Acts have been tentatively
identified (a Jerusalem-centered memoir behind Acts 1–5 and
an Antiochan source for Acts 6–12 and 15), source criticism
of the canonical Acts comes to a dead end with Paul's entry
into Europe in chapter 16. Luke knows of local traditions
connected with Greece, Palestine, and Ephesos, but the itinerary after Acts 16 is purely his own. We may correlate what
Paul writes in Rom 16:1–23 with his stay in Corinth in the
middle of the sixth decade of the first century CE, after which
point his letters provide us with no hint of his whereabouts,
his subsequent travels, or his end. Therefore, we have no reliable historical information about Paul after his sojourn in
Greece, which Luke begins to recount in Acts 16.

Luke has performed major redactional surgery on his
source or sources for Paul's stay in Philippi. Perhaps Paul's
career originally ended in Philippi with a fatal imprisonment
there; other local traditions of Paul's stay in Greece and Asia
Minor, of course, would be historically anterior to that final
incarceration. Data on Paul's peregrinations on both sides
of the Aegean may have been available only in fragmentary
local traditions at best. Luke has fashioned a narrative chronology that placed those traditions between Paul's Philippian
imprisonment and the travelogue of his extradition to Rome,
which all modern critical scholars agree is a Lukan creation
from its beginning in chapter 21 to its end in chapter 28.
Thus we have no sure knowledge of Paul after his arrival

in Greece, and the historical trail of his career ends in a Philippian jail.

A critical review of the attestations of Paul's martyrdom supports this admittedly provocative conclusion. First, sub-apostolic and early patristic testimony indicates the total absence of historically reliable tradition about Paul beyond his activities in the eastern Mediterranean. Whereas *1 Clem.* 5.5–7 claims only that Paul was a witness to ruling authorities, it stops short of saying that Paul was martyred. Clement is silent about Paul's stay in Rome, a curious silence on the part of a Roman Christian writing no more than a generation after the apostle's death. Clement says that Paul "passed away out of this world" after he had reached "the limits of the West"; this notice, however, only reflects a knowledge of Paul's intention to go to Spain after traveling to Jerusalem as stated in Rom 15:28, and suggests that Paul met his end there and not in Rome. Clement does not mention Spain by name, and there is no evidence whatsoever for Paul in the West,[15] unless we allow the testimony of the Spanish marionettes mentioned above. The notice is little more than an inference on Clement's part, and not in the least historical. The notice in the Muratorian Canon, an early third century witness, is also inferential:

> The Acts, however, of all the apostles are written in one book. Luke...includes events because they were done in his own presence, as he also plainly shows by leaving out the passion of Peter, and also the departure of Paul from the city [i.e., Rome] on his journey to Spain.[16]

---

15. See Helmut Koester, *Introduction to the New Testament* (2 vols.; Philadelphia: Fortress; Berlin and New York: de Gruyter, 1982) 2. 145.

16. In James Stevenson, *A New Eusebius: Documents Illustrating the History of the Church to A.D. 337* (rev. W. H. C. Frend; London: SPCK, 1987) 123. Latin text in Augustinus Otto Kunze, ed., *Patrum*

It is clear here that the Canon knows the "departure of Paul" (*profectionem Pauli*) not as his death but as the continuation of his apostolic journey from Rome to Spain (*ad urbe ad Spaniam proficiscentis*). In contrast to the report of Peter's martyrdom, the Canon claims that Paul escaped Rome to realize his stated aspiration to go west (Rom 15:24–25). Irenaeus claims that Peter and Paul preached the gospel in Rome and that the Gospel attributed to Mark was written after their "departure."[17] Many have interpreted this notice as a euphemistic reference to the death of the two apostles, but even if this is so, questions remain. Irenaeus does not say that Peter and Paul actually died in Rome, nor does he say that they were martyred under Nero. Early, unequivocal testimony of Paul's martyrdom, in Rome or anywhere else, is entirely lacking in early Christian literature.

The Pauline itinerary from the apocryphal *Acts of Paul*, reconstructed with some tentativeness by Wilhelm Schneemelcher,[18] also points in this direction. The apocryphal *Acts of Paul* treat those travels of Paul's least susceptible to historical verification: those corresponding to the Roman travelogue of chapters 21 through 28 in the canonical Book of Acts. In these Acts, the narrative begins in Damascus. Paul proceeds through Palestine and Antioch to Iconium and Pisidian Antioch, the locale for the so-called *Acts of Paul and Thecla*. Geography has here afforded a narrative fusion of traditions: stories of Paul and of Thecla are brought together in the common venues of Iconium and Pisidian Antioch.

Dennis MacDonald has shown that traditions of Paul suggested in 1 and 2 Timothy and in the *Acts of Paul and*

Ecclesiasticum Testamonia (Göttingen: Vandenhoeck & Ruprecht, 1848) 11.

17. *Adv. haer.* 3.1.; the Greek, ambiguously, reads ἔξοδον (exit).

18. In Schneemelcher, *New Testament Apocrypha*, 2. 218–33.

Thecla share persecutions in Iconium, Lystra, and Antioch[19] and involve some of the same dramatis personae: the ally Onesiphoros and the opponents Demas, Hermogenes, and Alexander.[20] Though we need not posit, as MacDonald does, that both the Pastoral Epistles and the apocryphal *Acts* have appropriated "the same oral legends,"[21] it is clear that the Paul and Thecla legends have undergone a narrative assimilation on the basis of shared locale. The apocryphal itinerary continues with Paul's departure from the region of Pamphylia to return to Palestine. The apostle then travels to Ephesos by way of Smyrna. The Ephesos episode ends with Paul en route to Philippi. The next episode, however, begins with a notice that Paul is leaving Philippi for Corinth. The section recounting Paul's activities in Philippi, which may have been of considerable length, is missing completely.

Scholars have been mystified by this extraordinary omission, hypothesizing that the section recording Paul's Philippian sojourn fell out of the *Acts of Paul* early and without a trace. I suggest that the Philippian episode was purposely removed because it was deemed unsuitable by the early redactors of the *Acts of Paul*. Many critics have noted that the *Acts of Paul* is a literary amalgam, pieces edited together but lacking in the narrative artistry of the canonical Acts. The redactor or redactors for these apocryphal *Acts* were less willing, or perhaps less able, to labor over the constituent materials in the narrative. They therefore included whole those materials they wished to weave into the text of the work, such as *3 Corinthians* and the *Acts of Paul and Thecla,* with little editorial reworking. Likewise, materials that proved troubling may have been rejected altogether.

---

19. MacDonald, *The Legend and the Apostle,* 45.
20. See ibid., 54–60.
21. Ibid., 45.

Such, I would argue, was the case for the Philippian episode. This section may have related a fatal imprisonment or
other local Philippian tradition that reported Paul's death
or at least the end of his ministry. Unlike Luke, the unknown editor or editors of the apocryphal *Acts of Paul*
found it easier to dispense with the Philippian material entirely. The narrative therefore could be continued with a visit
to Corinth and the obligatory terminus in Rome, where Paul
piously submits to execution. It is this terminus that caused
the redactional rejection of the Philippian episode: the hand
that gave us the Roman martyrdom narrative is the one that
took away the account of Paul's fatal trials in Philippi. Even
for the grandest of narratives, two martyrdoms are one too
many; even the great apostle is appointed only once to die.
In the final redaction of the *Acts of Paul,* that appointment
with death was in Rome. The rest of the narrative was then
redacted accordingly.

Everything that follows the absent Philippian episode in
the *Acts of Paul* shows signs of artifice. Paul's Roman execution at the end of the narrative is shamelessly fabulous:
that Paul's decapitated body spouts milk instead of blood
hardly adds verisimilitude to the concluding martyrdom account. The Roman martyrdom at the end of the *Acts of Paul*
is clearly a product of early pro-Rome propaganda, and it is
affixed to the *Acts* by the fabricated narrative bridge of the
Corinthian episode and the *quo vadis* tradition awkwardly
taken over from the *Acts of Peter.* If the martyrdom is later
than the other narratives that comprise the *Acts of Paul,* then
the *Acts of Paul and Thecla,* cited by Tertullian on the eve of
the third century CE, may not have contained a martyrdom
narrative. Western witnesses to Paul's martyrdom begin only
with Tertullian,[22] and his notice on the *Acts of Paul* gives no

---

22. See *Adv. Marc.* 4.5.

indication that the narrative he knew ended with a report of Paul's death.

Several other pieces of evidence, taken together, support a later date for the martyrdom. The Roman presbyter Gaius claims that "the trophies of the apostles" (τὰ τρόπαια τῶν ἀποστόλων) are to be found on the Ostian Way in the Vatican,[23] and graffiti celebrating the apostles Peter and Paul appear in the Roman catacombs no earlier than the seventh decade of the third century.[24] According to the fourth-century *Depositio Martyrum,* the Roman *cultus* of Peter and Paul was inaugurated during the Valerian persecution in 258 CE. Not until the end of the fourth century does testimony come down to us, in Jerome's *De viri illustribus,* corroborating the apocryphal story of Paul's martyrdom by decapitation and burial in the Ostian Way. The legend of the foundation of the Roman church by the apostles Peter and Paul became a powerful propaganda tool in the ecclesiastical politics of the late fourth century, which the Roman church wielded against the challenges of both Arian heresy and Byzantine pretensions to primacy. It is to this climate of ecclesiastical politics, not any historical veracity, that we must attribute the robustness of the Pauline martyrdom legend.

Eastern witnesses to Paul's martyrdom are later than those in the West, and more problematic. The fourth-century Manichaean *Psalm Book* knows of Thecla's ordeals in detail, but Paul's trials and tribulations are recounted without any explicit reference to his martyrdom.[25] It is plausible that

---

23. See Eusebius *Hist. eccl.* 2.25.

24. *PL* 23.617, cited in J. M. Huskinson, *Concordia Apostolorum: Christian Propaganda at Rome in the Fourth and Fifth Centuries: A Study in Early Christian Iconography and Iconology* (BAR International Series 148; Oxford: B.A.R., 1982) 83: *hic* [Paul] ... *pro Christo capite truncatur, sepultusque est in via Ostiensi.*

25. C. R. C. Allberry, ed., *A Manichaean Psalm-book* (Stuttgart:

the fourth-century Manichaean editors may not have known
of Paul's Roman martyrdom and were familiar only with
the *Acts of Paul and Thecla* without the martyrdom account. The testimonies of Dionysios of Corinth and Origen
are handed down to us by Eusebius, whose commitment to
the ecclesiastical importance of Rome must give us pause. In
the one place where we might confirm in an earlier source
what Eusebius says about Paul's Roman martyrdom, con-
firmation is not forthcoming: Eusebius tells us that Origen
mentions, among others, the death of Paul under Nero in
his commentary on Genesis.[26] But this reference is nowhere
to be found in Origen's commentary. And so Eusebius's attestation to the martyrdom tradition does not summon our
unqualified credence.

But where the literary witnesses are silent about the end of
Paul's labors in the East, the stones may indeed cry out. The
artifacts of the Philippian Extra Muros Basilica are of special
relevance to the question of Paul's martyrdom. In Crypt G,
a red-grained marble slab was discovered measuring 2.16 m
high and 0.86 m wide bearing the following Greek inscription bracketed at both ends with a Roman cross: "The burial
place of Paul, elder of the holy church of the Philippians.
Whoever puts another corpse herein after my remains shall
give an account to God, for it is a tomb to be used only
once (μονόσωμον) for a premier elder (πρωτοπρεσβυτέρου)."
Crypt G thus contains a memorial of a Christian leader
named Paul who died in Philippi.

Now, to identify this otherwise unknown presbyter with
the apostle Paul would be more credulous than critical. Certainly we would expect the tombstone of the apostle to

---

Kohlhammer, 1938) 143, lines 1–2. Thecla's trials are recounted in lines
3–9.

26. *Hist. eccl.* 3.1.3.

record that Paul was indeed an ἀπόστολος, the apostle to the Gentiles, and the apostle to the Philippians. But Paul's Epistle to the Philippians suggests that the expectation of an explicit mention of Paul's apostleship may be unwarranted. The Epistle to the Philippians represents several letter fragments, confirming Polycarp's later claim that Paul wrote the Philippians "many letters." In this amalgam of correspondence, Paul does not once refer to himself as an apostle, nor does he even mention apostleship. The absence of apostleship here is all the more remarkable because we would expect Paul to speak of his own apostleship in the autobiographical third chapter of the epistle.

Thus, though we cannot claim to have discovered the crypt of the apostle, we may have discovered an ecclesiastical memory of his life and death according to the Philippians. The vigor of this ecclesiastical memory also serves to explain why Philippi, after becoming administratively and financially unimportant by the third quarter of the third century, nevertheless became the home of three enormous basilicas clustered a stone's throw away from one another and nestled around a shrine configured in the octagonal pattern almost exclusively identified with *martyria* in early Byzantine architecture. The memory of Paul's martyrdom in Philippi may have made the city a place of pilgrimage, which demanded the construction of basilicas and a *martyrion* to accommodate pious tourism. It was on the Via Egnatia, not the Via Ostia, that the faithful were to find the final resting place of the apostle.

Ultimately, we cannot be sure how the apostle Paul met his end. But the story of his tribulations in the canonical Acts, the evidence of his letters, early Patristic writers, and the narrative of the *Acts of Paul* all pause at Philippi. I am not arguing here that the Paul buried in the μονόσωμον of the Extra Muros Basilica in Philippi must be the apostle who had exchanged letters with the Philippian church in the middle of the first century. On the basis of the evidence reviewed here, we can not sustain such an identification conclusively. This same evidence, however, even by its very silences and lacunae, suggests that our traditional picture of Paul as a Roman martyr is not a credible one and that the trail of the historical Paul grows conspicuously cold in Philippi.

General Index

Index of Buildings in Philippi

Figures and Plates

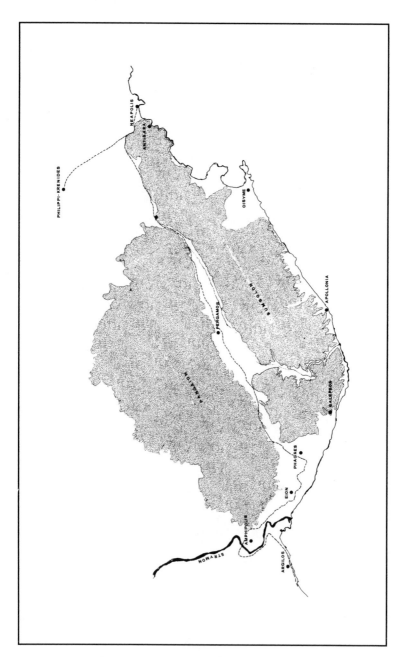

Fig. 1: Colonies of Thasos on its *peraia* (Philippi = Krenides)

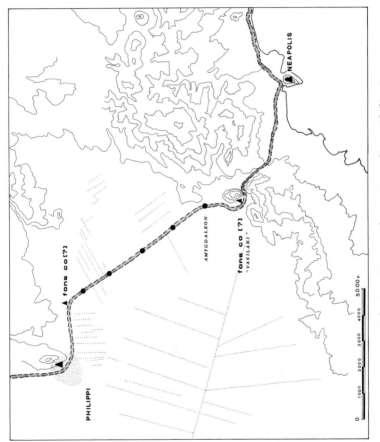

Fig. 2: The Via Egnatia from Neapolis to Philippi

Fig. 3: Plan of Philippi

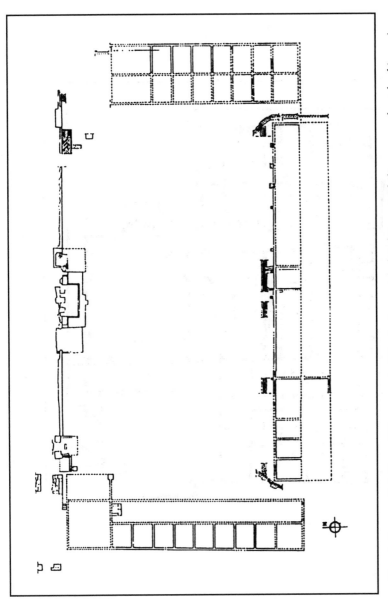

Fig. 4: Forum (M. Sève, "L'oeuvre de l'Ecole française d'Athènes à Philippes pendant la décennie 1987–96," *To Archaeologiko Ergo sti Makedonia kai Thraki* 10B [1996] 6.706, fig. 1).

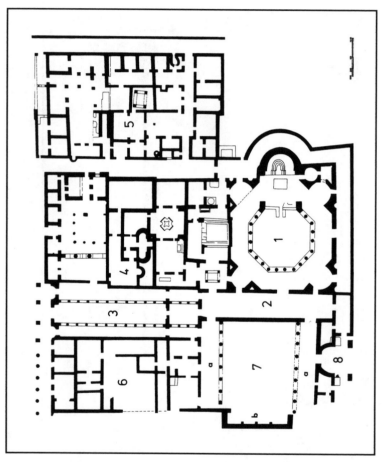

Fig. 5: The Octagon complex

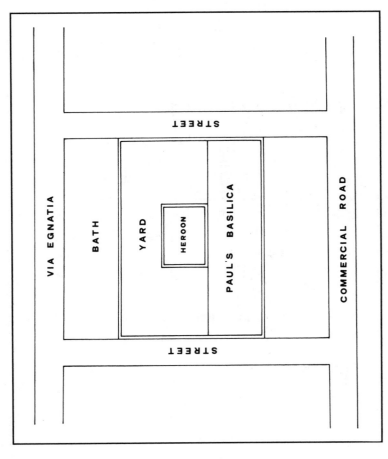

Fig. 6: The pagan heroon and the enclosed Christian assembly hall (Paul's basilica)

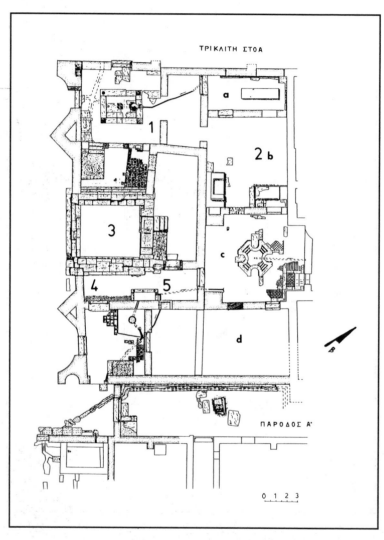

ΤΡΙΚΛΙΤΗ ΣΤΟΑ

ΠΑΡΟΔΟΣ Α'

0 1 2 3

Fig. 7: The northern annexes of the Octagon
(Gounaris, *Balneum*, 14; drawing prepared
with the care of Styl. Pelekanidis

PLATE I

I.1

I.3a

I.4a

I.2

I.3b

I.4b

Plate I.1 Bronze coin of Krenides. Reverse: tripod and the inscription ΘΑΣΙΩΝ ΗΠΕΙΡΟ ("mainland of the Thasians").

Plate I.2 Bronze coin of Philippi. Reverse: tripod and inscription ΦΙΛΙΠΠΩΝ ("of the Philippians").

Plate I.3a–b Coin of the Roman colony of Philippi, minted by Antony.

Plate I.4a-b Bronze coin of the Roman colony of Philippi. Obverse: Victory and the inscription VIC(toria) AUG(usta). Reverse: three *signa* (military standards).

Plate I.5 Medieval successor to the Via Egnatia linking Neapolis and Philippi.

PLATE II

Plate II.1 Stone well from a *mansio* ("way station") along the Via Egnatia between Neapolis and Philippi.

Plate II.2 Roman *miliarium* ("milestone") from the Via Egnatia.

PLATE III

Plate III.1 Monument of C. Vibius Quartus.

Plate III.2 East or "Neapolis" Gate. Tower.

PLATE IV

Plate IV Philippi, general view facing south. Center: Agora (Forum); foreground: Basilica A; left: Octagon and annexes; background: Basilica B.

PLATE V

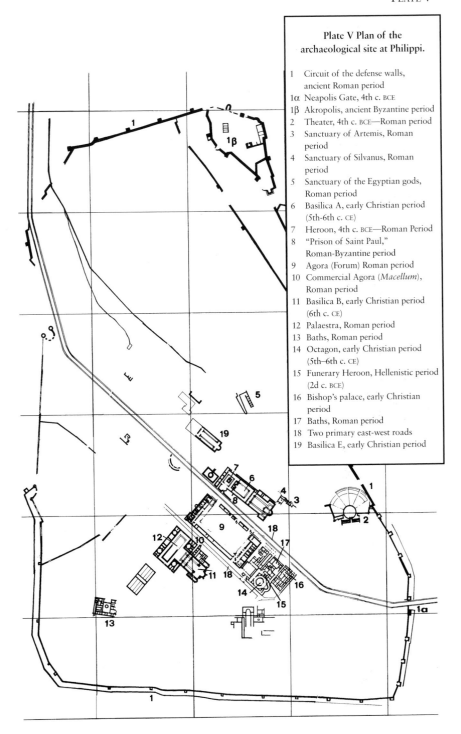

PLATE VI

Plate VI.1 Hellenistic streets to the north of the Via Egnatia.

Plate VI.2 Marble portrait of Lucius Caesar, the adopted son of Augustus (Philippi Museum, Inv. no Λ31).

PLATE VII

Plate VII.1 View of the theater from the north.

Plate VII.2 Temple-shaped building (heroon).

PLATE VIII

Plate VIII.1 Roman cistern, "Saint Paul's Prison."

Plate VIII.2 Reconstruction drawing of the monumental vault near the River Gangites.

PLATE IX

Plate IX.1 Hellenistic funerary heroon, subterranean burial chamber.

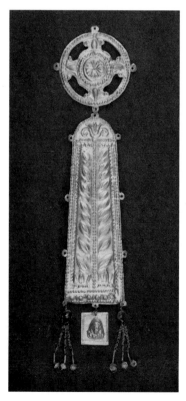

Plate IX.2 Gold head ornament from the subterranean burial chamber.

PLATE X

Plate X.1 Grave monuments outside the west gate.

Plate X.2a–b Bronze coin of Philippi, 42-54 CE. Obverse: Portrait of Claudius. Reverse: two imperial figures on statue base flanked by two altars.

X.2a

X.2b

Plate X.3 Roman bridge near Mavrolefki.

PLATE XI

Plate XI Marble grave stele from the west cemetery mentioning the Jewish synagogue.

PLATE XII

Plate XII.1 Justinianic impost capital.

Plate XII.2 Pavement in front of the northwest temple.

PLATE XIII

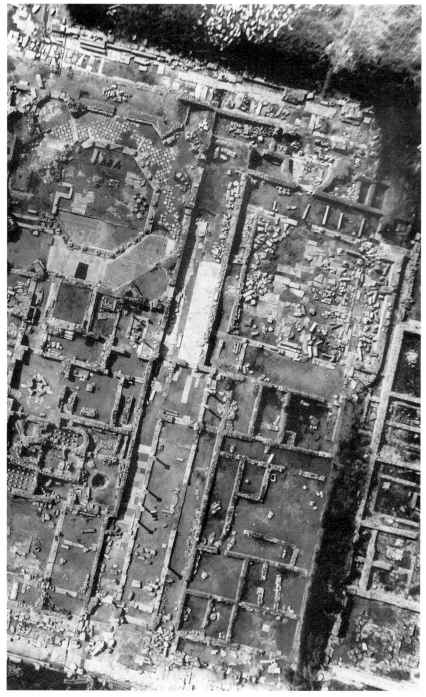

Plate XIII Aerial view of the Octagon annexes.

PLATE XIV

Plate XIV Aerial view of the Octagon.

PLATE XV

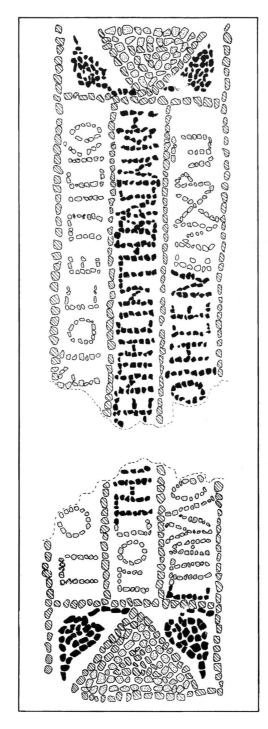

Plate XV Founder's inscription in the mosaic floor of the first Christian assembly hall at Philippi. Found under the floor of the late Octagon.

Plate XVI.1 Marble "constructed table" in the Octagon.

Plate XVI.2 Marble bollard from Neapolis harbor.